danc[ing]
with
crows

Gayle Baird

dancing with crows

Gayle Baird

ELYSSAR
PRESS

Dedicated to Olivia

Printed in the United States of America

First Printing, 2022
ISBN 979-8-9853686-1-1

Elyssar Press
175 Bellevue Ave
Redlands, CA 92373

www.ElyssarPress.com

Cover Illustration by Gayle Baird
Cover design by Stephanie Aoun Bou Karam
Book design and production by Stephanie Aoun Bou Karam
Book Art by Gayle Baird
Editing by Allie Rigby

acknowledgments

This book would not have found its way through me without the healing of the late Maestra Olivia Arévalo Lomas of the Shipibo-Conibo tribe in Peru. A heartfelt thank you to my friends at Allianza Arkana, and to Winston and his family for making that possible for me.

My writing was nurtured and encouraged by my family in France, – Sandra and Colin Bingham-Wallis. I am deeply grateful for their love, support and belief in me. My thanks also to Steven and Sandra Goldman, whose kindness and generosity changed my world.

Katia Hage, founder and publisher at Elyssar Press, has cradled this book since she first read it. She has infected me with her contagious passion and her belief in the power of our true stories to heal each other. She is an inspiration to me as a poet, artist, and publisher and one of those rare souls who has walked with me in strength no matter what storms arrived to greet us.

Thank you to the team at Elyssar Press and my editor, Allie Rigby. This book would not have come to light without Elizabeth Turpie, Patricia Delso, Graham Bell and Lachlan Grant, for their continued support and for reading my early drafts and encouraging me every step of the way. Thanks to Christopher McCullough at Exeter University, who saw the light in me and turned it up; to my partner John, who cradles my creative soul; and to my brothers, who keep me laughing.

Lastly, thank you to the rats, Blue and Balzac, who healed the inner child in me.

"A devil is a God which has not been recognised.
That is to say, a power in you to which you have not given expression.
You push it back and like all repressed energy it builds up and becomes dangerous."

Joseph Campbell

1.

I met Adam underground and underground we stayed. We ran from our shadows in the cracks of the masquerade that played out our days. I was starry-eyed. He was the night that gave stars a home, a night without roads and signposts, or places we could ever call discovered, or know.

We were crammed into the basement of Scotland's National Film School, waiting for the studio door to swing open and unleash our untameable life dreams. Our lecturers were late. The rest of us were wading in a sea of adrenaline that we needed to inject into something. We weaved amongst each other, broadcasting our charm with smiles too big for our faces. Adam didn't. Adam lounged nonchalantly against the door looking thoroughly bored.

I was unsure if it was him that captivated me or my fear of him. He was American, charming, and cucumber cool. But by the end of week one, he'd effortlessly unmasked the tutor's professional veneers and rendered them jabbering idiots. Sometimes it seemed almost cruel. When he didn't serve them back the opinions they doled out to us as facts, he laughed in all of their facades. I resented the arrogance with which he burst their façade of expertise and blew it up in all our faces. At the same time, I longed for him with a twinge of incurable lust.

We weaved around each other at the odd house party. Our few words became loaded. He seemed to reach through my skin and see the part of me that's most hidden, as if a separate universe existed for us that no one else would ever visit. His glare beckoned me into his mystery at the same time I heard the warning, "Beware you fucking fool, I might bite."

So I kept my distance until the wilderness of December on a film shoot on the Isle of Barra, a rugged, cold beauty of barren moors, rocky outcrops and turquoise waters in the southern Outer-Hebrides of Scotland. We seemed alone there, but for the freely roaming sheep and the white houses that strung out across either side of a soft, winding road, like pearls slipping free from a snapped necklace.

The land whispered a hundred thousand stories of the farmers, boat-builders, and fishermen that lived here, loved here and died here—or were forcibly shipped off to Canada to alleviate an over-populated island in the blight of a potato famine. In the hazy, violet dusk, a farmer told me about a young woman milking a cow in the fields by Loch na Doirlin, who was seized by the colonel's guards and forced onto a boat with nothing but the clothes that she stood in.

When the stories subsided, there was only a breath-taking stillness, the lapping of the waves, and husky cries of the sea birds. The rising sun dusted the hills in an apricot-tinted shimmer until the first glimmers of its amethyst descent. So beyond the crystal clear nights, the sky was permanently rolling in watercolours, dripping its silver-edged hues across the marshy carpet of sea-pink heather into the springs and the dykes that weaved down the hillsides.

We rose before the sun and bundled huge, hard cases of camera equipment, lighting, props and blankets into two, hired, white vans and bounced through the muddy fields to far-flung locations. Amongst the 14 cast and crew members, I wasn't sure what I was doing there. The director had asked me to crew because he liked my cheer, I think. I was credited as 'set manager' and mostly, I held things, took photos for my own amusement and wrapped the shivering actors in blankets.

Meanwhile, Adam framed their hopes and fears on 16mm film. He directed the camera team as if he was born for it, oozing quiet confidence and a confusing blend of patience and contempt for the rest of us. In the chill of the starry evenings we would huddle around the hearth in the cosy cottage on the hilltop and warm our chilled bones with the closeness of our sleepy bodies, while sipping on red wine and hearty soup. We watched old films, played poker and laughed like maniacs.

Niamh was almost always by me then. She was barely noticeable, but comforting, like the whispers of the breeze, or a sonata played on a piano far away. Niamh was half Irish, half fairy-tale. She had just started her journey in abstract painting at the art college after an aborted degree in English literature and two years of depression. Her voice was as soft as frosting and carried a lilting lyricism that soothed me like falling snow. She looked like the ivory femme printed on the little papier-poudre books of the early 1900s. She had the demeanor of a rose and the resolve of an ox. I cherished her. We shared a flat off Broughton Road with three boys and a mannequin. At my suggestion she'd been invited on the shoot to do the actors' hair and make-up. We shared a bed on the island, though I was too cold and too lusty to sleep.

One evening on that duvet, Adam played me his films. I fell into his fiction and found my longing. I thought I would never return from there, that home that disappears the moment I try to grasp it. I shivered with the stark realization that my feelings had slipped from my fingers.

Like amateur thieves, we slipped through the velvety dark and broke into the tumbledown barn at the bottom of the hill. The hushed, electric air of forgotten treasure enveloped the unlit jumble we walked into. I lay down on a faded olive green sofa embroidered with gold hummingbirds and I stretched out like a cat. Adam sat in a wicker chair in the soft pool of moonlight that streaked through the trees and cascaded through the window. We rolled a joint and smoked the last of his weed. We spoke of our hopes and dreams and the glass wall that we felt between us and society that gave us the uncomfortable impression we were somehow far, far away from everything. Our silences were pregnant with the world. He came to me and kissed me without asking, without needing to. We made love in hushed whispers like it was the only chance there ever was.

The next evening, in the indigo alley where night kisses day, we strolled together through the moors. He reached out to hold my hand at the same moment I skipped ahead of him. This was reflex. Hand-holding was risky and threatened my vision of everything. The way I saw it, I always wanted to be free. No one could hold me down.

The night-ferry from Castlebay back to Oban was rough and choppy. The wind whined of my lust and a longing to be held. The wall-lights fused out and rattled all night in their candle-shaped mounts. I couldn't sleep like the others, heaped together like seals in the cold and the sadness of an ending. In the early hours, I slipped out onto the deck and pushed my face hard against the howling wind that almost took the door off. Her icy shrieks and slashes devoured my cheeks as I pushed through the waves that were crashing over the boardwalk.

He was leaning against the railing like a part of the landscape, as velvet as the sky and as vast as the ocean. He took me under his coat and said, "So you found me." The tempestuous night sucked us into its vortex. I said to myself, "This is now. The beginning and the ending." The wind wrapped around us. We didn't move until the sun came.

After the Christmas holidays there was the mounting pressure to finish our screenplays. The ineptitude of the film tutors had begun to wear me thin. Niamh had met an Italian law student and spent most nights at his. I barely saw her. January was cold and miserable and I felt a horrific, unappeasable thing wriggling inside me, like a maggot that had sprouted my head.

I'd seen Adam once since Barra. I told him it was better if we kept our secret on the island, so people wouldn't make assumptions or imagine we were in a relationship, so we wouldn't think we were in a relationship. He agreed.

He didn't show up to lectures any more. I phoned him one evening when I was bored and alone. I'd ran out of weed. He picked up and said nothing.

"Hi." I said.

"Hi."

"What are you up to?"

"Nothing much, hanging out, watching a film."

"Do you want to come over?"

"Not really."

"Okay."

And that was that. I felt like I'd been stabbed in the gut, by something small, like a penknife. In a way, that made it worse. I suppose I wished it was more poetic, I needed a scimitar through my neck to give myself permission to feel wounded. A few days later I bumped into him in the library. He was browsing the shelves of DVDs. He greeted me as if I was a fart that had just drifted towards him from a backside that would never be identified. I wanted to ram him into the DVDs. Instead, I acted disinterested. I browsed the shelves, picked out two long, intense Tarkovsky films and left without saying a word.

Two days later I woke tangled in his sheets. It was already clear that his moods ebbed and flowed like tidal waves. I didn't know where he might carry me to and there was something magnetic in that. It was like travelling, in the beginning.

2.

I sit on his bed. I have one boot on and one boot off. I was going to stay, curl my legs under me. He has his back turned. He's jabbing a controller maniacally, tearing through corridors killing everything in sight. Our last words poured through kisses, poured through me like nectar. I'm still indented with his fingers, still drunk on him. That's why I'm here. I want him to kiss me, drink me, lick off the lies I tell myself and lift me out of the world.

He is fighting an interstellar war against a theocratic alliance of aliens in the orbit of a damaged planet, probably he is fighting his father. I am ripping the stub of a cinema ticket into a paper bird. He is bitching about the course tutors. Everything is wrong. I want to say, "Shut up and kiss me," but I don't want him to bite off my tongue. I feel like I'm suffocating. My body is tying itself in knots. I want to leave.

Is it true? This course is the worthless joke he says it is, that I've made a terrible mistake, that I ought to have taken that place at Oxford I so audaciously refused? Safer to ignore him, find anything worthwhile in my situation and milk it. He is talking at me with venom. I am staring at the door, at my boot that looks so pathetic on the floor. I am trying not to hear his words but they ring out like a public address system. He is telling me that after sex he is bathed in the clarity that his feelings were a pathetic illusion and he now needs to be alone. He is pacing madly and gesticulating like an orchestra conductor. He says it's always like this with women.

"I don't want anything from you."

My paper ticket is no longer a bird but a mess of jagged nothing that I extinguish with my lighter. I want to make it okay. I want to wait, but until what? Until things feel normal? Until I have conquered every longing I can't feed? I can't walk down the street with this feeling in my veins. I roll a joint. It was my unconscious habit not to get high before the sun died. That was then. I want him to see that I'm shaking. No, scrap that. I want him to see that I don't care. He doesn't turn around. The smoke wraps white and soft around my feelings. His angry mutterings canter over the hilltops.

Simone de Beauvoir walks towards me through the fog on the other side of the horizon. The fence between us melts away. What do I really want except freedom? Isn't that where we met and where we'll always be, in a conversation about Sartre and the wonder in his eyes that unfolded me in that moment and sowed an idea of him into my landscape? I wanted the freedom I felt on journeys, the adventure of fleeting passions, the total lack of tomorrows, the power of owing nothing and owning nothing. I don't want to lie underneath him. I put on my other boot and I leave.

Niamh is curled on my bed, her fingers stained with paint and blackberries. I am sketching her curves, which open to me, drawing me silently into the hushed world of symmetry where fingers and breasts are perfect shapes that fit together without question and I have no opinion about anything. A palm is four fingers. A foot is four palms. The shape beneath the clavicle is an equilateral triangle and between the legs. Two hands inside the thigh. The root of the penis measures up at half the height of a man.

My phone vibrates off the desk. I pick it up. Adam. I turn away from it to glimpse Niamh gazing out the window. Raindrops, a perfect nipple, erect, her chest rising, falling. Strands of hair kiss her neck, flyaway, effortless, free. I answer.

"What are you doing?" he asks, without a beat.

"Sketching. You?"

"Phoning you."

"I'm going to watch a film. Do you want to come over?"

He says nothing. Niamh is buttoning her dress. I turn to her.

"Don't leave. Stay."

"It's ok. I'm going to see Pete."

She pulls on her knickers, slinks out the room, closes the door softly.

"Who was that?" Adam asks me.

"Niamh. I'm..."

"No. I don't feel like coming over."

"Okay."

"I'd rather be alone."

"No you wouldn't or you wouldn't have called."

"That's not why I called." He says.

"Then why did you call?"

"Look. It's not you, okay? It's my medication."

"Oh. What does it do?"

"It's Prozac."

I breathe.

"It gives me these migraines."

We are silent.

"Are you depressed?

"No."

"Isn't Prozac an antidepressant?" I ask.

"Well yeh. I don't know. I hate taking it. It's my dad. The doctor prescribed it when I was thirteen."

"They're pretty strong though, I mean, if you don't want to take them it's your choice."

"My dad just insists."

"Could you talk to him about it?"

"Look I don't walk to talk about it. It's bipolar disorder. It's genetic. All my family needs it. I don't feel like coming out."

"Okay."

He hangs up. The silence buzzes through my empty bedroom.

I am visiting Winston, a Korean computer graphics student I met at a house party earlier in the term. He makes me laugh just by breathing. He has become my unofficial dealer.

"Drink?"

He pulls a bottle of bourbon out of the tiny cupboard in his bedroom.

"Not tonight."

"Beer?"

Two beers, strapped together with plastic.

"No. Thanks."

He looks hurt. I stare at the unmade single bed in the corner. It looks like a forlorn boat travelling downstream. Sometimes I need to lose myself. Sometimes I am already lost. I leave his house with a fat wad of weed warming in my pocket and step into the rain. The puddles join together on the sloping roads of Marchmont, forming one big river. I am wading downhill towards the meadows. In the playpark I will sit on the swing and rise above the houses. The rain soaks through my thin, camouflage jacket. I feel numb.

"Laila."

I look up. Adam is crossing the road in my direction. He has his hands in his pockets, hood up. He hasn't shaved.

"What are you doing?" I am staring at the empty menorah in the windowsill behind him.

"Walking back to mine."

"Where've you been?"

He nods towards the door I emerged from.

"Visiting a friend."

A motorbike headlight flashes across the puddles, blinding me, obscuring the street. The bike speeds past us, soaking my feet.

"You have a lot of friends."

"I lived here before."

"Right."

Adam and I walk hand in hand across the freshly cut lawns of the meadows where friends play Frisbee and students lie in the grass under the summer sun with half-closed eyes and books between their fingers. His fingers curl around my fingers. The warmth of his skin travels up my arms and shoots out my pores as we walk under the umbrellas of elm trees. It is a day for dreamers. They skip with guitars and manuscripts, the sun glowing through their faces.

"We're not in a relationship," he declared that night, and I too clung to the illusion that denying it made it unreal and therefore I was safer. I'd moved into his flat where we slipped out of sex-soaked covers into the outside world with the distant chattering birds of three in the afternoon. Now we were strolling hand in hand on the precipice of the world to the pet shop on Bruntsfield Place to bring home a hamster, which Adam named Broccoli Rob.

Broccoli Rob was placed under the window in the corner of the kitchenette where he would gnaw on the bars of his cage until a lump developed on his cheek that was half the size of his face. I cried for Broccoli, but I never held him. Not once did I open the cage. I consigned him to a world that was apart from me, as if he could be owned and therefore wasn't mine to love because he was Adam's. I said that caging animals was cruel and I wiped my hands of the matter. I suppose I believed that befriending him would make me implicit in his captivity and ignoring him would cancel him from my reality altogether. I didn't know then that the imprisoned stranger in that corner was a glass shard of my soul.

The bedroom is a smoky cave sprawled with our musings where it is always four in the morning and our conspiracies are drenched in candlelight. We travel on music into the ether. Adam sits in his ginger brown threadbare armchair by the window and I perch atop the bookshelves, dangling upside down to toke on his outstretched joint. The kitchen tap has come off its spindle. Neither of us can fix it. We live like children, eating tinned soup and adding brown sugar to all our hair-brained recipes. The walls are tacked with my portraits and paintings of nudes. The long shelves in the kitchen are lined with Adam's empty boxes of cookie crisp. In this gingerbread house of neuroses everything is good and possible and my own flaws are also my magic. The symmetry of his boxes comforts me, a protection from the chaos of kitchens where china is displayed and never drank from, where shelves are lined with leather-bound compendiums of Whitman and Blake that have never been read, and I'm prohibited from touching. Here I am safe from a world where I am demanded to sit now, don't speak now, nod timely, smile widely and laugh politely, suffer privately, defecate silently, and agree willingly or you're sickly and deranged in the head. The cardboard corners of Adam's cereal boxes recede and approach like a train of carriages in a toyshop that I could poke into oblivion and nobody could stop me.

Yellow wallpaper is sagging off the bathroom wall like a sail riding on the wind. I dance naked in the shower, washing pans and singing to my mixtapes. My mind is a screen playing scenes for the screenplay I am writing for my thesis film. The door opens. Adam is home with groceries. He laughs and climbs in. We sing and soap each other with bubbles. I speak in French. He picks me up and we meet against the wall where a spider is weaving her destiny. We travel on a high-speed train that bypasses so many stations. We no longer kiss on the mouth. He says it's too intimate. I pretend this is mutual, which is easier than admitting I'm falling for him. I pretend a lot these days.

In his bedroom, I am fresh from college and making film notes. My bum is wet from my bike seat. He is pacing back and forth across the room, gesticulating wildly. He's on one of his frenzied, oratorical rampages. The candle tongue is huge and flickering madly. I finish a sketch and ask him to take a look. He perches on the chair arm and hunches over the shot-list I have mapped out for my film. I have asked him to shoot it. This week we are officially friends and sleeping together. This is an official meeting, or not. I drop my lighter and bend under the bed to reach it. I find a condom wrapper.

"There's a condom wrapper under your bed."

"I didn't use it."

"It's been opened."

"I said I didn't use it."

"Don't insult me."

"It was just some girl I met."

"Where?"

"At the pub."

"Was it good?"

"Yeh"

"Was she nice?"

"Yeh. She stayed. We talked."

I went to my room. I did have my own room. It was the size of a cupboard and I never slept there. I don't remember how the argument went. I remember him following me, I remember cowering in the corner of my bed while he raged above me, thrashing his arms like a thunderstorm hailing abuse. I remember my fear while I was choking for breath, thinking he would hit me, wanting him to, begging him to. The physical sting would numb my agony. He broke down in tears and told me that she'd been a prostitute. He said he needed a woman he couldn't hurt. It wasn't the first time.

"I hate myself!" he screamed, broke down and wept.

I held him as he rocked. He described how it felt to spend days in euphoric rapture only to wake up with a girl beside him and feel revulsion and disgust. He listed the girls he'd caused so much agony, girls who'd never forgive him, girls who went mad wondering if they were completely deluded. When he was high he was oblivion: I fell into him and just kept falling. I flew for days without landing. Falling was flying if you never hit the bottom. But I did hit the bottom, smack on my face.

When he felt low, he'd insult me. The bruises started small and swelled into ruptures. Eventually they consumed me. He kicked me like a ball. Every time I clambered back to my feet his verbal boot cracked open my face and down I went again. He hurled a tirade of abuse while lighting matches, throwing them down at me as I scrambled on the floor with singed, black hands, desperately choking the parts of me going up in flames. The more resilient I was, the more brutal his attack. He yanked me by the hair and scraped my cheek across the floorboards, across the glass shards that shattered where he threw away my years. It seemed all he wanted was to crack my resilience, wear me down until I was nothing individual, not even human.

When every ounce of self-respect I'd ever lost and regained had been annihilated, when there was nothing left of me but body fluid and the need to be held, then he could embrace me again. He kept striking until I got there, until I reached the edge, beyond the threshold of pain into a euphoric white light that was total surrender. Then he was there to pick me up and claim himself my saviour, the only thing safe to place faith in. He'd wipe away my tears and rub my nose with his nose. He changed roles before I had time to feel how I felt and adapt to my pain or grief or relief the fight was over. Drugs didn't help, nor the traumatic high from starvation. I didn't have my body to guide me.

When I was a pallid wreck, drowning in my own fluids, horrified by the gunk streaming from my face, that's when he found me the most attractive. He'd flip in a dizzy instant from a beast into the lover I recognized, a sailor who'd been lost for days at sea, dewy with the gentleness that only comes from staring death in the face and surviving. Then I'd admit to myself that I'd missed him to the furthest edge of grief, beyond which I saw only a void. We held each other like shipwrecked brothers and fell as one into the wave of our tears. We washed up as children, naked and laughing. Then lust would plunder over the sand dunes. Charm and seduction came like Bedouins swathed in exotic thobes emerging from the distant ocean-mist riding camels. He'd flip me over and fuck me. He could no longer touch me and look me in the face. For him I was merely a receptacle. I no longer existed. This was the choice I didn't realise I made.

I knew nothing of who I was anymore. I thought this was the prize of his acknowledgment I'd endured everything to reach. I told myself I was a warrior and that this relationship was only a swinging gauntlet that I was learning to dance with, that it never really sliced me to pieces. I thought to say "enough, I give up" would be to admit my weakness, that the more I could endure the stronger I was proving. The obstinate resilience I'd always believed was my greatest ally was the demon that tore me to shreds. I stayed with him like I stayed with anorexia, believing that I didn't deserve something healthier, something better.

I also believed I could wait long enough for him to change, for him to love and let himself be loved. I thought I could save him without drowning. But I was drowning. I didn't tell anybody. I was unwilling to admit that I couldn't make it work. I walked out into the smoke and snow of the city with broken bones, welts and bruises all over me. But there was no trace, no evidence, and no witness, only a story in my head.

He convinced me that nobody cared for me, and that every person and activity in my life was somehow a dangerous threat, except him.

He drew me a route on a map and filled my car with petrol. But I drove it. I steered myself down that road that would lead me away from myself, from my friends and my dreams and anyone who might convince me to change direction.

He played the role of a psychotherapist who would heal me. He lectured passionately on how he'd conquered his own mind in the past. I knew this past was some imagined place. I witnessed his silent struggle in the present every day. I knew that he turned me into a movie screen where he projected in real time all that he was claiming to put behind him. But I lived a double life too.

The kitchen is full of our college friends. Adam slides towers of poker chips between his fingers. The clinking is steady, like a grasshopper. In the corner Broccoli Rob gnaws on the bars of his cage. At the poker table, Marcin shuffles. Zogo hands the beers around. Nicolas munches a bag of jelly sweets, half of which have fallen out his pocket and cascaded down the stairwell. I notice them as I lock my bike and run up the steps, wet and high after teaching swimming.

I change into a skirt in Adam's bedroom, pull down a blue ceramic dish from his top shelf and count the pills inside. Three. I put the dish back and search the room for a plastic orange bottle. I find it on the shelf above the fireplace. The bottle is labelled with his name, the address of a US pharmacy, and in capitals: ADDERALL: AMPHETAMINE SALTS. I pour a few into my hand and zip them in my purse. I break one open and swallow half its powder. For sleepless weeks I have been a lightning-bolt riding horses bareback in the clouds.

I join the men in the kitchen where I am welcomed with grins. I pour myself a strong drink, roll a joint and choose some music.

The game begins. My horse has wings. I gallop in the hoof prints of poets on a trail at the edge of the sky. "We are the music-makers. We are the dreamers of dreams." Their stanzas become my heartbeat. I know when to jump off the cliff edge, when to fool them, when to ride. I see the cards before they're shown to me. The boys are afraid to tango with me, except Adam, who joins me in the dance just to flaunt his lack of fear. But I can see through his fearlessness straight into his pride. I know when to take him down. When he has a hand that can't be beat all his masks fall off and bare his innocence. That's the only Adam I ever thought I knew.

Almost every night now the boys come over to our place. I am one of the men, and also I can't be. I have a cunt we're all aware of. Night after night, my chip stacks dwarf the poker table and I stroll out with the money. I am on a winning streak. It lasts for months. Adam stares at me with unblinking fawn eyes. His long eyelashes are dark and thick, accentuating the mysterious feminine charm that mates his wild machismo. None of us are completely fooled by it and yet all of us are magnetized. My manoeuvre is dangerous but I go all in because I feel it. I am surfing adrenal waves. Without a beat's hesitation, Adam calls. He has two pair. On the turn the dealer flips a queen. I land a straight. He pushes back his chair.

"She's insane. I can't play this shit with her. She makes ridiculous moves that have no strategy. It's not even poker, it's just a kid's game. What's the point?"

The guys fall into an awkward silence. Everyone is staring at me. He throws the remainder of his chips across the floor and storms to the bedroom where I hear him punching the walls.

"It's my deal," Marcin says, and we try to play on as if nothing happened. Awkwardness has crept into all the cracks. It wasn't the first time. It wasn't the last.

I see them out. He's playing Halo. He has clothes pegs hanging from his nose and his ears, an ice pack strapped to his head.

"Are you okay?"

"No. I have a migraine."

I'm thinking, "Don't treat me like that in front of them. No fuck that, don't treat me like that ever."

I say, "I'm sorry."

"What's going on with you? Do you have a deal with the poker gods?"

"It's not about the cards. I'm playing the player."

"No you don't, you're just insanely lucky and you keep hitting."

"No more than you."

"That's bullshit and you know it. They give you the nuts and me jack shit."

"You sound crazy."

"Yeh, well I feel crazy here. Does no one else see what's happening?" He grabs his head in his hands.

"It's not normal. You're making me question the laws of reality."

"I'm going to bed."

"Go."

I take one of his sleeping pills and my nightly Prozac, the anti-depressants I have finally yielded to after years of saying "not a chance" to a string of medics who peddle the wares they have doubtless never even licked let alone swallowed. But they have fact sheets, they reference medical bibles. Oh yes, biblical certainty, full-proof, Byzantine facts. Adam gave me the nudge, sugar-coated them like macaroons. Tonight, I lie in the single bed in the cupboard and I sweat.

I wake in soft covers. A car engine purrs over the soft tick of his heartbeat. Headlights slide across the ceiling and disappear. I tilt my chin and arch my back; the stretch shoots something close to honey through my veins. The cotton between my toes is a new pleasure, and these dark corridors of open-eyed delirium in the night. In my sleep I chase my ghosts with buttery toast up a Marchmont stairwell; liquid stairs blur tears in my eyes and make stars in his candlelight. He lives in the dark, showers in the dark; sleeps with heat and the hum of a fan. It sculpts new shapes in the smoke cloud. I must breathe more deeply. Adam's bed, we entwined mostly here. I pushed him in the heather last December when we drove out to nowhere to find a wild abyss for his film-set; he laughed and pulled me down. But in the end he needs routine, control, and a need to make me hate so he can seduce me once again.

I am looking back on my sunless summer, a season shrouded in the mournful semi-darkness of a daylight I couldn't wake up to and an eternally undefined time. I polluted the bed with dreams I couldn't reach. I woke up tired and empty, my eyes full of sleep. I'd been too deep and couldn't breathe, couldn't reach back and shake myself into feeling. The depths of my distance filled the room from floor to ceiling, shrouded the bed. I rarely made it out before lunch.

I rarely ate lunch and rarely ate. I stopped running, stopped dreaming, and started sleepwalking like a zombie sadomasochist through a depression I clung to as if it was integrity of feeling. Most artists are depressives, I told myself, and smiled grimly in the belief that without pain and self-annihilation there would be nothing to write about and no reason to write.

And now I laugh my stupid face off in the understanding that it was too dark to write anyway. I barely had the motivation to pull down the toilet seat, never mind pick up a pen. I felt pain, yes, in some indistinguishable region of my body, but otherwise I felt nothing, no ground beneath my feet, no wind in my face, no hunger for food or sleep, for sex yes but not for passion, the pain was too numbing. The sex was entirely impersonal.

I suppose that's why I liked it, because I didn't want to get closer to me any more than he did. He rejected me daily, recoiled at my touch, barely kissed me, licked me twice in twelve months, fucked me seldom and never when asked. He did it wildly, with passion but not affection, on average, once a week. And just when I was giving up on myself, he was there to make me wet and lick the tears of my lament. I thought, at the time, he felt stronger to see me weak. I had found someone that wanted to hurt me as much as I did, and that was as close to understanding as I felt I'd get. It is easy to wonder why the hell I didn't leave this. For a while I believed his words and rare fucks were the only thing keeping me from peeling my face off with lit candlesticks. I thought he understood me, if not my body. I thought I'd just arrived but admittedly I'd been losing light since I left Lombok. It's been over two years. He guided me through the dark and into its heart. I suppose I was drawn to him so I didn't have to wander there alone. At the same time I can say, now that the fog is clearing, that I've been hiding from myself for most of my 26 years. Adam's denial helped me see this. He led me to confession and I pulled him in with me. I will not regret him for this.

3.

I crawl out of his covers at 6:00 a.m. I don't know what day it is. Time no longer has meaning. Speed is a jet engine that circles the globe without landing. Dappled rays of sunlight fall through the meadows. I retrieve my clothes from his armchair and cycle into the mist, past the morning joggers and dogs sniffing flowers and each other or leaping after branches. I stop at the shop to buy some breakfast. The aroma from the bakery is the dance of the morning. On the way it was on my mind, "Will I? Won't I? No I won't. You can't. You won't. Stop it you bitch. You've tried. You've failed. I'm stronger. Shut up. I always win. Fuck you. I'll just come back to hurt you later. Make life easy. Shut up you crazy bitch." The trees shake, shimmering with dew drops, they look like a memory, the past behind glass. The conversation in my head hurts too much. The fighting voices are torture. I just want peace. "Fuck them," I say and walk into the shop smiling.

The Danish pastries and croissants are fresh from the oven and still steaming. The baker slides a silver tray of apple turnovers and chocolate plaits beside me. Devilishly, I pick up the tongs and I slip them into a brown paper bag. Not one, not two, but five of them. My heart is beating fast. I have perfected this art. My skin becomes eyes. In the next aisle I slide them into my bag. I know where the security guard is and every shopper in the place. The camera watches me. Who watches the camera? How fast can I move? I find the ice cream, the chocolate, everything that's sweet and soft and forbidden.

I have nice legs, blonde curls, a short dress and a bright smile. I watch myself through their eyes. They probably think I'm stupid. I look so innocent, just an object to be seen and not heard, another mindless blonde. I am proving them all wrong right before their eyes and they don't even know it. My world is a parallel universe.

"None of you can see how fucked the state of the world is," I am thinking as I picture myself setting fire to the diseased heart of society. My clandestine life is mine and mine alone; if they can't see me they can't define me. I pay for a head of broccoli and some apples, chatting brightly with the lovely lady at the checkout. I'm shitting across all their categories and they're eating me up. I wish "good morning" to the security guard and stroll out the sliding doors into the powerful wind of a new day. The shock of adrenaline is my morning tonic. I ride it all the way home. I know I make a fine bandit because I've done this every day for three years. It hibernates my hate so I have only love left to give. I am the love child of Jesus and Satan and fuck the prim, proper young lady my mother and her mother wanted me to be.

I fill a pan with boiling water, lock the door to my bedroom, turn on some music, and start the race against my metabolic rate and the

outside world. Like a tiger tearing up an antelope I devour the pastries, rip the thick kilo bars of Swiss milk chocolate from their foil wrappers and break them into the boiling water. I stir them with a spoon into a creamy chocolate sauce and plonk in the ice cream. I shovel big dollops of melty, chocolatey ice cream down me with a spoon, pick up the pan and I drink, drink, drink. Then I hide the mess of wrappers under my bed, storm to the bathroom, shove my fingers down my throat and I puke until there is not a drop left in me.

Afterwards the silence is like music. The queen could walk into my house and punch me and I wouldn't feel a thing. My heart beats soft and fast. The world is cleansed.

When the guilt and the shame set in. The only thing to do is to do it all again. Broken shards of liquor bottles collect raindrops on the muddy slope outside the supermarket trolley park. Men and women in anoraks huddle at the bus stop, rolling cigarettes and scratching at lottery cards. I'm wondering where all the lost dreams gather from these people and if all my thoughts are excuses I make for an eating disorder, or if an eating disorder is the excuse I make for everything.

Everything is fucked. A bloke called Frank is sleeping in my bed. I close the door softly and leave, cycle into the night and pedal towards Adam. Drunken men stumble over the cobbles of the Grassmarket laughing and crying in each other's arms. One of them is singing about Angels. Niamh and I have moved into a new flat. I feel like I'm living in a goldfish bowl. When I look out my window I meet the lost, ravenous eyes of the diners shelling prawns on the café veranda opposite me. The room is pregnant with all the people who lived and possibly died here before me. In this goldfish bowl I can't sleep, so I have been bringing home Marcin and Teo, a love triangle sparked by strong hashish, Polish vodka and a threesome.

Teo has no interest in Marcin so it's not really a triangle. Her fiery Romanian anarchism warms me. Except beneath it she's soft and too clingy. She's put me on a pedestal and I know that soon enough the bird's-eye view will bore me, and one day I'll fall off and break my ribs. Also, she seems to be trying to convince me I'm a born lesbian and the cock is only a diversion. Marcin speaks little and when he does it's off the wall. Our silences deepen my curiosity in his tiniest movements. What worlds I can conjure in a jaw twitch. He remains a mystery, which is probably what attracts me. He has a girlfriend. I choose to make this his own responsibility. I care for him, which is becoming a problem for me.

Meanwhile Adam's silence is louder than I care to listen to. I'm trying to get over him by distracting myself, but he niggles in at all the edges. Frank has travelled up from Manchester to sound design the film. He is a professional. We met at a fence beside my film school. I have developed a habit for these kinds of meetings. Frank is balancing levels and laying sound effects over the edit. That is not why he came. I discover this in the kitchen as I peel my way out of his arms. I was never very good at rejection. This one feels like drowning a kitten.

Teo wants to see me. Marcin wants to play. I can't bare it any longer, which is why I am cycling away from the situation. I feel trapped in a city that refuses to be new again. Every street throws me an old memory, until I reach the junction they call The Pubic Triangle, where strippers on their fag breaks flaunt their wares, framed like renaissance paintings in paint-chipped doorways.

Most days the zone swelled towards me and swallowed me. I call it a zone. You could call it a trance. I'd wake from my nightmares and it was in my bed beside me, crawling through my window and impregnating the room. Some mornings I woke and felt the zone on top of me. It reeled me out of bed and into my clothes. Before breathing my first breath I was already taken, already possessed. The orders were wordless if I just obeyed. When I questioned the hunger, the overwhelming hunger, the need to binge and purge every thought away into oblivion, things got nasty. That's when the zone showed her face and struck at me with fists. All that crap about my rebellion and cunning, that was just the shit I told myself to keep the fists from stabbing. Sometimes they had daggers, sometimes butcher's hooks. They writhed like snakes in my belly and hissed at me in tongues.

So it was easier to surrender and enter the zone without struggle. I moved in a bubble that funnelled around the well-worn tracks of my purging routine. Everything beyond the bubble seemed faded at the edges, distant, unreal and inconsequential. Bumping into a friend, an invitation, an obligation. It all faded like the end of a sentence you don't want to listen to. This was the only obligation that mattered, the only one I could make time for without punishment. A comforting white noise muted out all sounds, most deliciously the sounds of my own thinking. The people around me swirled like paint strokes. Afterwards, I'd starve myself until the next time. With a routine there was less need to ever hear the screaming.

But later, my routine descended into chaos. When I couldn't handle a situation, like when I visited my father, I would puke five times a day. I screamed through every second of it. I screamed at my ribs clawing out my skin, I screamed as I cycled once more to the shop and bent over the toilet bowl, at the thoughts lashing me on, punishing my appetite and the aching, grinding hunger in my bones, my muscles eating themselves up, my body devouring itself. I screamed at my every thought, my every action. I hated what I was doing. I had always hated it. Suddenly the noise was deafening, the thoughts I'd always heard but muffled, the wailing of emotions I'd invited the trance to suffocate into oblivion.

Purging always came second, after months or years of fasting when I had become too ravenous and angry to prolong my hunger strike.

4.

The white world crunches under my feet. It is his sound.
Matias, a film student at my new college. Snow falls softly. The
pond is frozen. A hushed whisper. Swans huddle in a corner that's
still moving. They look somehow different, less sovereign, and
slightly pathetic. I run around them and up a little crackling trail
that winds to the peak of Arthur's Seat, the sleeping volcano that
peeks over the city. Light drips in gold columns, landing in a misty
halo that coats the sparkling, silver heather.

Scenes of my past are churning under the rocks and slipping
down the hillside, scenes of whimsical sex, men who wanted just
a glimpse into the mystery, all my could-bes. Maybe it was what I
was looking for. I forget that I'm running until I reach the tribe of
squawking crows that spiral around the rocky summit. I feel safe
here amidst the clouds that sweep around us and elevate us from
the city. Down there it looks like a picture in a pop-up storybook
nestled by white and purple hills. The landscape winks like an old
familiar mirror.

I stand on the tip of the volcano suspended in clouds and inhale
all that is fresh and good and safe. Smoke rises from the chimneys,
trailing snakes and ladders through the sky. The city exhales. I'm
out of reach.

I fly down from the volcano into the pages of the city's book with
my wings stretched out like an eagle. When I reach the fence that
splits the wild grassland from the criss-cross streets of Georgian

houses, I am overcome with nausea. I bend double and puke across the virgin snow right there on the border. It is the fourth day in a row. Two months earlier I was reclining on a chimney pot above the rooftops of Calcutta, floating in a sea of stars and satellites. They promised me a future I couldn't see yet. I felt it pierce the night sky and stretch across everything, reaching towards me, asking for my hand.

I needed to come back here. I needed to leave Scotland to know the earth is still spinning. Matias is chatting to Julio on the hotel roof beneath me. My film school compatriots. The 2:00 a.m. breeze is warm, but I have goosebumps. My body is watching him watch me. I've been bending backwards over the railing of my bedroom balcony, letting go of my hands, and looking for the courage to just fall through the city. It's lost to me. At the Satjit Ray Film School, I am directing a short film funded by the British Council.

We float through the school's lush gardens on a tiny white path that trickles through the orchids, over the lily pond, past the cricketers. A group of Indian film students are weaving amongst us, smiling intensely. They lead us to the cinematography building where three 35mm cameras whisper of a world I once fantasized. I am introduced to the art director who will build and decorate our set in one of the purpose built studios. I am called with the crew to the school directors in the top-floor boardroom where I am cross-examined by a room of sharp, interrogating eyes. Sketches are studied, a script is broken into lists of shots and props and call times. Actors audition. I rehearse, I direct, and I envisage fragmentary somethings. I pretend I know what I'm doing, that I'm not grasping in the dark for an ephemeral truth that ever eludes me. I stepped into the role that breathed fear through the bones of the three men studying and working with me. I wrap that around me like a blanket.

I once said I'd rather fail spectacularly than feel ordinary. Maybe someone else said that. In any case, the saris flitter all around me like tropical birds. I am floating in the omnipresence of the country I fell in love with, playing feels safe where magic exists.

On the evening before filming begins, a swelling tide of students and faculty collect in the tiered auditorium of the college cinema to watch the screening of our previous films. The room smells pleasantly of saffron, tamarind and dust. I am already accustomed to the scent of Indian cinema, its unabashed spice of melodramatic emotional climaxes that seem obscene and overpowering to my penchant for subtlety. Still I find it almost unbearable when the violin strings slide in, as if we humans must be zapped with a defibrillator to feel something. The scenes are giant gobstoppers in my throat, refusing to be swallowed.

By the time my own chilling soundtrack chimes in, I am almost choking. I start shaking and close my eyes. In the deafening silence of the auditorium I'm sure everyone can hear me screaming. Before it is over I slip out the room and I run. I run up stairs and through corridors to the darkest corner I can find. The confident girl that I present shatters at my feet and echoes through the drainpipes. I fall down and I weep. Every film I ever made was a spectacular failure, I weep for every one of them. I weep because it isn't funny anymore. I weep because I let down my cast and my crew. I feel soulless and fake. I constructed crude and empty caricatures. It hurts to look at them. I weep uncontrollably into the liquid glass of the taxi window all the way back to the hotel. My sobs are muffled by the monsoon downpour. My shaking is felt by everybody.

I spin in the breeze on my balcony replaying the scene. Matias came to me. He wrapped his arms around me and gave me his belief; a faith carried away in the streaming gutters of Edinburgh art college. He lifted my falling bra strap and replaced it gently on my shoulder, whispering of the kisses he'd like to place there and of how much he'd wanted me.

"It's killing me" he mumbles breathlessly, "If only, for tonight, Chivon didn't exist."

Chivon's his girlfriend. "Yeh, right", I think. I wrap Indian silk around me and go to my room.

Over the rooftops I see Jono, the cute Yorkshire surfer I met in Sri Lanka. Behind him I see Olle, the Swede I fell for on a Balinese boat in the Indonesian ocean. I see Kim and Lena and Matthew. They were surfers and artists and poets: everything I needed and everything I dreamed of. All my lovers had girlfriends. At some point I asked for this, behind my own back. Are love and freedom really incompatible? My reveries are disrupted by the high-pitched ring of my mother phoning me at university when my stepfather threatened to leave her.

I remember the industrial cheese grater of her wailing, the bleeding, the sting, "What am I going to do? Where will I go? I can't. I can't be alone. I can't. I'll die Laila, will you come and save me if he goes?"

To rescue my mother would mean drowning myself, going under

as I did all those times I tried to save her in the past. As it turned out, my stepfather stayed and I didn't need to drown or even flail in her riptide. Instead, I dumped my boyfriend. Now here I stand on the Indian balcony of my hotel bedroom, missing Adam, sobbing and phoning him.

The next day, with filming over, we are free to explore the city. The market is as potent as an acid trip. The colours swirl towards me. Live eels jump out of buckets, spiralling upwards like the smoke from metal urns and the cow dung. Decapitated pigs's heads wink from bloody tables. I am dwarfed by giant heaps of chilies and spices, tobacco and mangos, peppers, pomegranates, bananas and roses. Men gather around card games and chess boards perched on broken crates and moped seats. Women robed in all the colours of the spectrum heave their way through the chirping, bulging throng for silks and ingredients and hair slides. Chai is brewed in giant cauldrons. Battered balls and rings sizzle deep in the oil of big woks. Midriffs wink and eyes sparkle in shells of charcoal. Big cream cows with bells roam around the fringes sneaking bites of fresh lettuce. Matias trails me with his camera, filming me. He says it's a cinema verite exercise, which I find amusing.

Back in Scotland it is my first visit to the main campus. I float down the corridor with a dancing lilt in my steps. I just smoked a joint in a park around the corner. Also, morning sex has this effect on me. Walking beside me, James Mavor, my writing tutor, broadens his shoulders. His neck sinks into his stiff, olive tweed suit like a turtle inching into its shell.

He suggested we conduct our first tutorial in the college canteen. I am flying high on passion and too excited to argue. He leads me through the crowded dinner hall to a small, square table in an unexceptional row near the centre of the room. We seem to be beached in a sea of white plastic. A group of young, teenage students saunter past us in tiny mini skirts. He stares there while I stare at the large, glossy walls painted a nondescript colour between yellow and grey. He clears his throat and strokes his wiry, ginger beard.

"Well obviously you're not a writer."

He lifts his coffee, offering a pause long enough for me to sink into or retaliate. I look away from him to the distant window that frames a corner of skips in the back lot of a construction site. The view is too far away to be an ally, but I try to make it one.

"You wrote the film you directed for the art college didn't you?"

"Yes."

"Yes. The writing was problematic."

The writing was surreal. He sips his coffee, leans back and puffs his chest out, apparently waiting for me to say something.

"I know."

"You may well know that Matias writes and directs his films, but that's extraordinary. He won't have it any other way, but he's an auteur like that, a visionary. We have many highly talented writers studying screenwriting here. We can organise for you to meet them and read some scripts."

"Actually, I already have ideas. I'm working on a draft of the screenplay."

"Right. We're not keen on students entering the course with their own ideas and naturally, we highly encourage collaborating with talents in their own field."

"Yes but I have to follow the flow of inspiration."

He sighs.

"What is it then?"

I have this habit of fluttering my eyelashes as if I'm deep in REM. when I speak. It's embarrassing and uncontrollable, especially when I'm nervous.

"It's set in a dressmaker's shop on the...."

He laughs.

"Will the characters be dressed in outlandish, theatrical costumes like your last film?"

I don't speak. I stare blankly into his stiff, brown tie and smile.

"Look I don't know you yet, so I'm really not sure how I can help you. Have a think about it and let me know when you want to see some scripts."

I cycle home to Adam's in fury. The sky is raining baby dragons. When I enter Adam's room, I brush them off my coat but they scramble up my legs and crawl all over me, breathing fire across the room. Adam is kind. He stokes the flames and adds logs for me. He wants me to assert myself. I tell him I don't understand why the rage doesn't register until after the event. At the time I felt nothing. I'm an automaton, smiling sweetly, acting only to please, agreeing on reflex.

"Who is that imbecile who possesses me?" I ask.

"I don't even know her."

I woke in a dusky apricot fog, licking dreams of Matias from my lips and my eyelids. It clouded me all day, hovering timelessly, nestling into tree branches and the gaps between my toes. I caught glimpses of the present in its holes, a seagull the size of Pavarotti masticating a Big Mac, Adam's erection mirroring the phase of the moon and trying to tempt my clothes off.

The fog left the city around 10:00 p.m., at which time I was cycling my cold, sorry ass and the scent of chlorine across a violent sea of traffic and the semi-naked fairground that I usually avoid and hence forget on a Friday night. In Charlotte Square, amber and emerald flashing liquid magma pulse through my bus-horn-headache and the raindrops in my eyes. A downpour of inebriated fuckers living for the weekend, hunting for a dance, for clairvoyance in the dark, for sauce on their kebab or fellatio from just about anybody. Scottish whisky, nasty cider and fingered nuts raining down inside my mind, a wet mind and wet hair, icicles at my nipples, Matias gazing back with wide eyes, depthless reflections of my idiotic, romantic idealism. Whimsically, he would like to fuck me but not to know me. I am no stranger to this wilderness.

The sky mirrors my bedsheets, a washed-out white which suggests a below-par water temperature and a lack of imaginative sex. Nothing wants to be here. I can hear the scuttle of snails leaving their shells from my bed. For weeks and months the sun has gone missing. Prozac is a grey bubble that carts the world away from me. This dreary pigeon-shit sky dribbles over everything. It clings to my pores, hovering, refusing to just fall and wash the scum away.

Disillusionment stalks me everywhere. It drips inside my boots as Oscar lights my fag outside the screen academy. I've started smoking, a rebellion against my exercise obsessions. Oscar is one of the three male lecturers. He leans over me, discussing a personal film project he is trying to persuade the world to finance. Oscar exudes the will to fuck in a way that makes me feel he's torn my clothes off, like the man who undressed me in the meadows this morning while walking hand-in-hand with his girlfriend. Sometimes I hate having a cunt. I savour the burn of the cigarette in my throat. It feels better to feel something. Matias strolls around the corner and halts beside us. We try to voice words but they leap noiselessly from our lips and suicide bomb in stringy puddles. The tension is observed by all the potted shrubs. Someone opens the door for us. We step inside.

Every second week we stand on the podium and present our filmed assignment for the fortnight. I used to stand tall. My legs are weakening. I have unwittingly entered a talent show officiated by underachieving despots who lounge in their seats sipping bitter instant coffee from tiny plastic cups. It is becoming harder to hold my head up. I try to circumvent their grim, redundant critiques but the truth is I can't. Instead I tell myself, "I will suck it up, I will make the best of this." I am here to show my mother I did not need to get a "real job."

James likens my exercise to a memorabilia Princess Diana doll that his wife has. He seems to resent the poor bitch. He brings her up every time we speak, as if he needs her indirect presence to comprehend me as a woman. I want to talk film, but he jabbers on about his self-sacrificing position of cradling her through spasms of depression. He drivels on about her like Adam would describe me, with an unmistakable twinge of self-pride that says, "She needs me." His pity makes me want to puke all over him. I don't know what his point is about the doll because he doesn't make one and in any case I'm trying to drown his words out. Up there on the podium what I hear is "useless, maudlin hysteria" while I am scrawling in huge capital letters across my notebook, "Wake me up from this nightmare. Wake up. WAKE UP!" I can't see the ink because I have pools in my eyes but whatever I'm writing it's supposed to be a cue for my tears to fuck off. I will not let them see me cry. I will not give them the entertainment. Screw it. Screw you James. I'll come back next week with a shotgun and blow off your testicles.

Matias invites me to coffee. We walk to a baroque, Chilean café in Bruntsfield. He says they're friends there. I stand at the bar while Matias chats with the owner. I don't speak Spanish but I speak the language this man's face speaks. Matias looks embarrassed. He leads me to a booth by the window.

"What was that about?"

"I shouldn't have brought you here. He knows Chivon. He thinks I'm, you know… Cheating on her?"

"It's just coffee."

"Exactly."

"James was harsh. He's always harsh to you."

"I'm not the only one who's noticed?"

"Every week he idolises me then tears you to shreds. It's embarrassing. I don't agree with him about your work by the way. Your piece was really good this week. Is that why you run, to run away?"

"What do you mean?"

"Was that guy Adam?"

"I run because it feels good."

In the filmhouse café James scoops up my script and leafs through it as if it's smeared in dog turd. With every page he turns, fury flashes its fire through his eyeballs and his cheek skin. One of us is going to combust. For my benefit he feigns the impression of looking for something in my pages and finding them vacant. He pushes his spectacles to the end of his nose and looks down on me.

"I really can't see what you're trying to say here. Also, you have more than one protagonist, which never works."

"Emi is the protagonist."

"Remind me. Who is Emi?"

"The little girl who gets hit by her father."

"Well what's the point of the other women? Because all I can see they're serving to express here is a great deal of sexual frustration."

"It's not that. It's stages of life, how their lives intertwine, affect, and reflect each other. Emi's innocence, Grace's hope, Clea's wisdom."

"I just don't see how we can relate to any of them. Is Emi a happy or a sad character?"

"Both. Neither. Her emotions shift."

"She has to be one or the other. Your writing's just all over the place. There's no clarity."

"She... I was happy when I came in here," I say, turning silent.

"I think you need some help. This just isn't working."

I say nothing.

"How is your home life?"

"Hard. Fine. I'm fine."

My eyes well up.

"Some days my wife just can't take herself to the doctor. We have a neighbour that drives her. Would you like..."

He reaches out and rests his hand on my forearm.

"Excuse me."

I push back my chair and rush to the female toilets. Inside the cubicle I fall against the door and I weep the kind of tears that choke all the oxygen from the air and croak in strange voices that resound like alien toads from some distant galaxy. I'm petrified by these noises I don't believe I'm capable of making. I hear a toilet flush and turn silent. A door creaks open. Three footsteps. A tap trickling pathetically. I hold my hand over my face and read the poster on the door about chlamydia. The hand dryer relieves us both. My silent witness leaves without a word. I inhale deeply, tear at the toilet roll and blow my nose. In the mirror I splash cold water on my face, rub away my smudged mascara and lean into my reflection. I stiffen my jaw and stare fiercely into the eyes I know so well and don't know at all.

"Get it together. You will not let them drag you down. You will not care for their approval."

Months later, I am standing on another stage in the plush lecture hall of the art college. In this old haunt I once sunk into snippets of film history and begged myself to find all that was endearing in the fiction lecturer's fascination for celebrity gossip. Today it is my turn to stand on the podium. We are pitching our films to a room full of teachers and students as an examined assessment and a plea for crew. I enter the inner calm I can find on a stage but not at a dinner table. I screen a trailer and present my outline. I make them laugh and I make them feel something. I feel it too, emotion rippling, surging and crashing over a sea of heads. As I open the floor to questions I respond to the three men's familiar pokes with convincing eloquence.

"There are too many protagonists in this story. A story needs one hero."

"The little girl is the hero and central to the action. I'm showing how our lives intersect and have a domino effect."

The art college staff praise me. I feel proud of myself. I even convince myself I am confident.

After the last pitch draws the event to a close, a dozen students approach me, compliment my work and express interest in crewing my film. I catch myself soaring weightlessly into skies strewn with stardust, the galaxy opens to my belief. I am becoming the filmmaker I set out to be. The last time I felt this, I was filming. I am lost in this reverie when a throat is cleared beside me. James. He's been lingering near me for the opportunity.

"Laila. It seems you did quite well. God knows where you pulled that one from."

I stare him straight in the eye. We are ushered into the drinks reception in a glossy walled conference room. Trays of wine are whisked around by the two networking officers who greet me with characteristic affection.

"Laila. I wanted to tell you some of the actors from your art college film were in the screen academy the other day and they spoke so highly of you. They were reminiscing on the workshops you led prior to your last film."

"Thanks Clare."

I meander through the throng, joking and laughing with many of my old acquaintances from the art college. I am chatting with Nelson, a flirtatious Argentine on an ERASMUS scheme, when my eyes meet Matias watching us. There is another pair of eyes on me. I've been feeling them for the last half hour, an itchy, squirmy feeling. It is by accident that I found them. Boring into me from the wall. James Mavor standing alone, a glass of cheap Merlot clutched tight between his fingers. My glance is momentary. Just a flicker. But enough. I feel his jealousy as if he threw the whole glass at me.

"You were getting on well with Nelson."

Matias is beside me.

"Yeh. He's hysterical. He always cracks me up."

"He likes you. So does that other guy you were talking to just now."

"Ivo? We're just friends."

"Don't play naïve, it doesn't wash with me. Your pitch was great by the way. Well done. You showed us up again."

"What?"

"Hugh and I. You're the prize student. The only one of us they all have faith in."

"So far from the truth."

"Ask Hugh."

I am slightly drunk by the time James sidles up beside us. I am talking to Karen, a woman who works for a film talent acquisition company. After he speaks she floats away, calling a name out, and leaves us facing each other.

"Great person to know." He says, "You ought to meet her colleague Kim, she might be useful to you. I know her well. I can introduce you if you like."

"Oh I already know her. I met her last year and we've been joking about work experience ever since."

His whole body has a momentary seizure.

"Well I'll stop trying to introduce you to people then."

The phlegm bounces off my shoulder. I wobble on my footing, rendered totally speechless as I try to process the realization that I just witnessed him throw a tantrum and transgress the codes of social decorum I always claimed I despised. I am too shocked to commend him.

I offer a slurred, "Right" and walk away.

5.

In the pub named The Blind Poet I am drunk, swaying gently on the bar stool like a wild oat in the breeze. The pub is packed with a clan of regulars. The tiny round tables are crushed close together making us all one big family. Van Morisson's "Sweet Thing" is playing through the speakers. I feel the leer of men's eyes crawling all over me.

"They're all looking at you," Matias eyes them and eyes me.

"I know."

"I want to take your clothes off right here and right now."

I turn away from him towards the bar man, who looks up from the beer tap and grins at me.

"Do you have anything less romantic?"

"I'll have a look." I turn back to Matias.

"That's nice Matias but I'm thinking of Chivon."

"What?"

He can't hear me over the music and the drunkards.

"I'm thinking of Chivon."

"Chivon's none of your business."

"My guilt is my business."

"It's not for you to feel guilt. You don't know her. You're not friends."

"Maybe we could be."

"You couldn't."

I try to listen but my body's speaking louder. I'm doing mental arithmetic with my thoughts as if I can balance the equation.

What do I think? What do I really want?

"I tried to call you the other day but Adam answered the phone."

"Really?"

"He said it was an unrecognised number."

"I deleted you."

"You're such a kamikaze, romantic, Antonioni woman."

"I didn't want to think about you."

"Did it help?"

"Not really."

"Adam told me not to call you again."

"What?"

"He said, 'Is this Matias? Don't call her.' Then he hung up. I guess you told him about me?"

"Yes. We talk. We're mates."

"What did you tell him?"

"Not much. I didn't show him your erotic texts if that's what you mean."

"I think you'll get together again."

"We tried. It doesn't work between us."

"Why?"

"Let's not talk about him."

"Well I think you'll get back with him."

"Not likely."

"How's your script going?"

"I've written fifteen drafts and they're still not happy."

"Well, they're backing you. You're still the golden one. They've given up on me."

"That isn't true."

"Are you still writing about the little girl?"

"Yes."

"I don't like films about children."

"The 400 Blows?"

"Don't like it."

The door creaks open, blasting us with icy wind. A couple shuffles past us, unbuttoning their snowy duffle coats. A group greets them with cheers and back pats. Matias shuffles his stool closer to me to give them space. Someone drops a glass. It rolls on the floor but doesn't smash.

"How's yours going?"

"I'm not writing. It wasn't working and you want to know why? Cinema Verite's hooked me. I don't want to try to say anything. I mean, what have we got to say? I'm going back to my hometown in Spain. I know a prostitute there. I want to spend two months with her, capture something of her life."

"Why?"

"She's human. We're not so different. I want to know, to understand. I'm a Catholic."

"What if you can't use another as a medium to your understanding?"

"But what if I can?"

"Hmmm."

The next thing I remember is the snow crunching under our feet. We stop to roll a joint under the canopy of a big oak tree. He's telling me he wants to bottle the falling snowflakes in his sound recorder, but they make no noise. I know they do, if you really listen. But I don't say this. I'm wondering if he's bottled me there, words I spoke in Calcutta. He's warming my hands. The moonlight licks his face. It is difficult to find anything worrying in a white world without footprints. The snow blankets all our lies. He pulls me into him.

"I need to kiss you."

"I can't."

"Why not?"

"I can't, not here."

"We're alone."

"But these are my meadows. If I kiss you here, you'll change them. They'll always be the meadows where I kissed Matias and every time I come here you'll be here too."

"Isn't that a nice thing?"

"No. It will hurt."

He takes me back to his house. The joint was too strong and I feel dizzy. The walls vibrate. Matias says he feels sick. He shows me into the bedroom. "Our room," he calls it. I am not the second party of this we. He leaves me there and goes to pour us a drink. I hear the bathroom door click shut and sit down on the bed. White sheets. I think of her. I wonder what she's like. She looks wispy and pretty in the framed photos on the drawers, like an Irish fae. I imagine she's nice. The room is beginning to fill with my past lovers, sauntering through the walls with cheeky, carefree grins and charming whispers. I am reasoning with myself. If every guy I'll ever like in this world cheats, then I refuse to be a doting girlfriend believing in a love that is something it isn't. He told me he's cheated on her before. She knows. She forgave him. If there's no love without lies then fuck love. I don't need it. Fuck men. Fuck Adam. My jeans are wet and cold. I take them off, lie on the bed and wait for him. The bedroom is neat. There's nothing to look at that isn't her. I hear him puking. Maybe I should leave. My longing for him is like a heartbeat. Before Calcutta I'm sure I didn't have one.

He's standing at the doorway with a face drained of colour. He looks like a helpless boy that needs his mother.

"I was sick. The joint was too strong."

"Are you okay?"

"Yeh. You look... incredible."

A wave of nausea crashes over me. I run to the bathroom and puke. In the mirror I look fine, I think. I'm here. He's here. Didn't I want this?

At 4 a.m. I am lilting through the snow with a song on my lips. The world is untouched and with me. A thousand curtains are closed.

Matias is no doubt staring at the bureau drawers wondering in God's name what he just did. Behind the curtains the rest of them are up to all kinds of unspeakable things in the dreams no one else sees. Meanwhile, the faces of all those strangers now are as innocent as newborns. I have left him to lie in the bed that we made and I am back in the meadows, which are forever changed by a winter's night when I didn't mean to kiss him but I did.

My skin is singing a homage to caresses. My soles kiss the snow. You don't realise you've been missing something until you're so full you're bursting over the treetops. I want to lie down in the snow and roll like a pony.

He's there all the time, under my skin and my bones, like an echo that's more real than the him I remember. I taste him in a place I can't locate, a place I didn't know was of me. This wanting could wrap around the universe a million times and still go on unravelling. I want to lick him from the trees and taste him once more on my tongue. I know not to want him. I know not to like him. I know he's a cheat and a liar. I know I'm no better. I just can't help it.

It's Friday night. The boys invite me to the pool hall. I decline. I walk up to college to join Nick's film club. The streetlights glow amber and hum in quiet whispers. Nick is the technician. Soft. Artful. Endearing. The one staff member I enjoy seeing. He's a good friend of Matias. He warned me away from the course before I came here, promised me that the teaching was bad. I didn't listen. He's showing "The Passenger." Matias sits at the far wall amongst a jovial crowd. I don't know any of them. I sit alone. I always liked going to the cinema alone, floating anonymously in an ocean of strangers. Outside, the frost gnaws my face and through my tights. I smoke a cigarette and warm up with thoughts of the waves off West Timor. The film lives on inside me, to be loved and not held down, to be life's passenger. The pavements are glossed with black ice. Walking is a lethal exhibition as the passers by show me. He greets me at the door.

"Hi."

"Hi."

"How was it for you?"

"Antonioni knows me."

"I don't mean the film."

I look at him. I look for him. His crowd crosses the road and calls after him.

"We're going out for drinks. I'd invite you but Chivon might join us later."

"Bye then."

I walk home across the ice sheets, wondering why I left my

bike behind. I wouldn't mind toppling over the handlebars for some kind of sensation. The journey is endless. I'm bored and tired of this stupid, fucking pavement. For the first time since the beginning of university, I see the path as I saw it before I etched it with my memories. I came up to Edinburgh for the open day. I stood in the swanky entrance hall of Napier's plush film school building feeling as inconspicuous as a flamingo. I drank their punch and read the glossy handouts they splurged around us. Men in suits guided groups around state-of-the-art studios. I felt like my limbs were disengaging from my body, like I'd paddled out of my depth and the current would swallow me. A friendly networking officer directed me to the art college, where their sister courses were run, explaining there was no ceremonial schedule of talks and events there, but a receptionist I could talk to. As I walked that road the tears started streaming. I couldn't understand why I was crying except that I was a moron. I felt awful and everything seemed wrong. I lashed at myself for being so pathetic. "Suck it up Laila. This was the dream, remember!"

Yes, this was the dream. Filmmaking was the dream. The place at Oxford was my mother's dream. I slip on the ice. As if time slows down, my bending torso and helicopter arm swings save me from crashing on my face. I look around. The streets are empty. Nobody saw me. The path saw me. Why did I think I knew better than my instincts?

At home Adam wants to fuck me. He points to his erection like a five-year old kid who just discovered his Christmas presents.

"You won't want me again tomorrow."

"Don't say that. Don't imply I don't care about you."

"You said you don't."

"You're changing my words. I never said that."

"What then?"

"I care about you."

"Because of Matias."

"You deserve better."

"You don't want to be with me, but you don't want me to be with anyone else."

"It's not like that. I can't control this genetic affliction. I'm not normal. If I had the choice I'd always have an erection."

"That might get awkward."

He's crying. I hug him. He's warm and I say,

"I'm sorry Adam. It will hurt me too much when you don't."

I go to the doll-sized room I unthinkingly call mine and lie down on the single-bed that is squashed against the wall. Matias saunters through my mind, skiing across the ice with Chivon. I toss and turn for hours that feel like days, unable to blink them away. I stare at the whispering window and see him beyond the rooftops. He is merrymaking all over the city. I don't care. I don't care. I curse the lumpy mattress and the claustrophobic walls of this stupid, tiny bedroom. I try to jerk off but it hurts. I can't bare it any longer. I crawl out of the duvet and go to ask Adam for one of his sleeping pills. He wakes to find me wrapped around myself in his armchair, staring out the window. I'm reading Balzac. He says I just walked into his dream. I say I just walked out of a wormhole. I read to him from Le Père Goriot,

"The most heedless passer-by feels the depressing influences of a place where the sound of wheels creates a sensation."

I take a pill and lie with him. He turns over and spoons me. At some point in the night I wake to find him peeling off my knickers. I let him. He enters me. I feel slightly paralysed, sleepy and dreamy, lapping on a sea in a vortex between worlds. I couldn't move if I wanted to. My cunt feels disconnected from my body. I feel used. It feels better, like a home. I sink into the velvety, moist black of its womb. He kisses me on the mouth for the first time since Barra. The interstellar dust is still floating.

In the morning he wakes early to catch a train to Glasgow where he teaches a cinematography class. He's late and annoyed, muttering about a broken night's sleep. Through crunchy eyes I watch him pull his clothes on and grab his camera bag. I'm losing sight of the scene as dreams gallop me away. The door slam jerks me awake. The emptiness of the house reverberates. Snow keeps falling, hushing the world away. I'm languishing in my underwear, watching lonely walkers plod beneath me. My days fragment like the people, broken, in mutiny, crying out for a better author, for some kind of continuity. I'm wondering where the people are going. I want to know of their fears, the last thought to make them cry or laugh or feel loved. I want to discover what makes them fall in love with life. I feel so adrift on my lonely island.

A fat seagull is giving me the beady eye from the nearest streetlamp. I grab my camera and start snapping, if nothing else to propel me out of my mind and into the present. This makes her squawk like a lunatic. A second gull lands beside her and joins in the honking. A third glides over the rooftops and grounds on the streetlamp opposite. I can only assume he's their chief by the way they regard him. Also, he's enormous. The three of them are squawking like an out-of-tune organ and the church choir of my school days. I know something is afoot when another three gulls dive-bomb from a chimney across the road and circle speedy loops towards my face like torpedoes. The chief dovetails for my camera, wailing savagely. He's going to plough through the fucking window. At the last breath he swerves. His crew latch behind and soar on to their next target or home to the shores of the ocean. I don't know what the devil that was about, but it felt like a warning.

6.

It feels like a joke, like a terrible, humourless joke. I can't make it feel real. I'm sitting at the doctor's desk in a windowless room painted the insipid green of sterility. She smells of a miserable Scottish day, like biscuits and leather. She smiles widely. She has lipstick on her teeth.

"Laila, Laila, Laila. What are we going to do for you today? I hope there's something we can do. Have you heard back from the eating disorders clinic?"

"Yes I had my interview. They said they couldn't help me. I want an abortion."

She smiles, not even a flinch.

"How long have you known?"

"Since yesterday."

"Maybe you want some time to think about it?"

"I've thought about it."

"This is entirely your decision. I know it's not an easy decision. We have maternity counsellors you could discuss your feelings with."

"I don't need one. I don't feel anything."

"Are you sure about this?"

Of course I'm sure. I'm a wreck. I want to delete it before it has time to grow and attack me. For now, I can still tell myself it's not so different than some jissom splurged on a pillow. It's no doubt already warped beyond restitution with my melange of narcotics and destructive psychoses. And its mother would be me. What chance does it have? I want to nip it in the bud before all hell breaks loose.

"How's the Prozac going?"

"Terrible. I can't sleep. I can't wake up. I can't orgasm. I can't feel."

"We could try upping the dose?"

"Your colleague already tripled it. I'm done with them."

"Shall we try another? It's a lucky dip you know? How about Venlafaxine? That's a nice word."

I wince.

"Tell you what, keep taking the Prozac for now and we'll talk about that after all this is through. I'll refer you for a termination at the royal infirmary. They'll call you to schedule the appointment."

What makes people think that I'm brain-dead?

"Tu veux le petit-dejeuner? Un pamplemousse? Un croque-monsieur ou un petit-pain avec le confiture de framboise?"

I am running my fingertips down the soft groove that slices his torso into chambers of symmetry. Chambers I've understood, in some other time and some other place. My French accent charms him. He laughs and kisses my breasts that are swelling at a rate I find miraculous, like a time-lapse of springtime. I am sick all morning, all afternoon and all evening and craving tastes I've forgotten since I banned them from my world when I was twelve.

The changes in me happen quickly. They feel playfully novel, curiously astonishing, for a day or two. We observe them like amateur physicians. Then my appointment is made and Adam books tickets to visit an actor in London. He says he needs the

actor's voice-over to finish an edit. The edit has been unfinished for four months and at this
moment he's decided four months is too long. I think nothing of it, just as I think nothing of the fact that we're sharing the same bed once again or that there's a tiny being swelling in my womb. Instead I watch the snow melt, revealing thick, nebulous wads of congealed, black leaves. I quit my job. The boss rams me out of her office. I don't get my final pay cheque.

Adam leaves. Niamh's too busy to see me.
"I've been at a wonderful party for three days with dear new friends near the Beecraigs. Spending the weekend with David," her text message informs me. I throw my phone at the door. I don't give a fuck if she's snowed under in the Transantarctic, she could still offer a semblance of caring. She's been too busy since I told her I'm in trouble. I start to cry. She's too scared to face me. Glittering a dog turd and handing it to me as a gift only makes it more insulting. I phone her and tell her this. We start to shout. Niamh, the soft as candyfloss charisma, the sister-in-arms I still love, shouting at me.
I never thought we had it in us. She hangs up. It's my own fault really. She always shuddered at my insinuation that sex and procreation were not pieces of angel cake. When Niamh and I attempted to find mutual ground on matters of love everlasting, we were like two rabbits trying to bone through a wire cage. It is possible, but mostly just awkward.

The days drag by like tired cart horses. I find Broccoli Rob dead in his cage the night of Adam's departure. I can't bear to touch him so I leave him there. I suppose the cage-gnawing addiction took him in the beginning. My bike is stolen from the stairwell by some punk I'll never have the pleasure of castrating. I walk the slushy paths up to the screen academy for my board meeting, the official go-ahead for my film. I puke in a bush outside the Evangelical church. Paul, Oscar, and James greet me in the corridor and guide me into the boardroom where they have a rranged plastic chairs in a circle. They dressed up in tight suits and labelled themselves financiers for the occasion. I sit beside my producer and we impress them with our production file and my tits, which are five times the size they were last week. This has them gawping at me with faces like mullet fish. It hardly seems reasonable to offer an explanation.

Walking back to the house it is impossible to ignore that the mullet fish have washed up on every street. I want to squash every leer in the direction of my mammillae and scream "don't you know what these are for?" It occurs to me then that I am completely and totally invisible. For how long have I been kidding myself? I don't want to be gaped at. I really just want to feel love. The drizzle falls faster and fiercer, I lift my hood against the spit and collide with a man rounding the corner.

"Sorry." We speak at the same time. He steadies me from falling. I look up into the face of Matias. He takes his hands off me.

"Where are you going?"

"Home."

"Adam's?"

"Yes."

"How have you been?"

"Fine. Good."

"Really?"

"Really."

"Where are you going?"

"My board meeting."

"Good luck."

"How did yours go?"

"Well. They gave me the go ahead."

"Are you sure you're okay? You don't seem okay."

Maybe it's the rain, or the hormonal chaos. My eyes fill with tears. I hate that he can see that. He hugs me.

"I'm pregnant."

It blurts out before I can catch it. He pulls back. His pupils dilate and dart in all directions at once.

"Is it mine?"

I hadn't considered that. Adam was at home when I pissed on the stick. I just assumed. My belly screams. I realise I'm aching all over. I try to do the math in my head. The days roll into one. It's hazy. It could be.

"I'm not keeping it."

He looks away.

"I'm running late."

"Go."

"Call me if you need anything... if you need support."

I nod, turn and sprint through the rain. I wouldn't call him if I was in the paroxysms of an anaphylactic seizure and his was the last number I had.

I've run out of speed. I've run out of weed. I can't bear to leave the house. I stare out the window as the thunder claps in the meadows with venom. When I was a kid I stared out at the same pastures as they rolled past the car windows. They looked so lascivious then, a fairground of strangers with curious handbags full of secrets, all striding on their separate ways with the purpose reserved for the clandestine lives of grown-ups. I tried to imagine the stories of the realm of the epic city. I knew only the farm, a manic-depressed mother, kids in nappies, dairymen. I had nothing whatsoever to go on. Now I was one of them. This wasn't where I was supposed to end up.

The bus pulls up. The hospital doors are crowded with smokers, paramedics and wheelchairs. I follow the alphabetical signs through endless corridors, sign in at the desk, take my plastic cup and my forms and wait in the airless annex. How do they suck the life from these places? Some kind of deadly nightshade in the ventilation system perhaps.

A teenage couple in tracksuits sit near me. She lies in his lap, face full of make-up and bubble-gum. He's scratching his balls and playing with his phone. They seem comfortable here, as if they come here biweekly to lunch and it's an entirely natural place to be. A slightly older girl sits with her mother. The girl hides her blotchy face in a glamour magazine. Her mother sits stiffly, sallow and possibly paralysed, like a domestic cow doped on opiates abandoned on the moors in the twilight. I want to prod her to see if she's really alive but I notice she's still blinking. I leaf through the forms on my clipboard. How much do I drink? How much do I smoke? There is comfort in the reminder that I'm unfit to vessel anything.

The man dressed in white is angry with me. He says I didn't drink enough water.

"I drank the specified amount."

"You couldn't have."

"I did."

Maybe I didn't. Who knows anything these days? They go through with it anyway.

"That was nothing," I think when I'm back in the house re-writing the sixteenth draft of my screenplay to meet the demands of the apathetic teaching staff dressed up as executive producers. Three runaway trains of conflicting advice from said producers crash and self-detonate. The notes of my script-consultant flap about like stray leaves of bog-roll in the ashes. My head hurts. I can't find a way through any of it. I read back on what I've written. The inspiration that sparkled through the first draft has vanished. The rest splattered out the ass hole of something. I don't recognise any of this. I shut down the document and play online poker. I lose. I keep at it until I've extinguished all the funds in my account.

Later it hurts. It really hurts. It hurts so much I want to scream. I don't even whimper. Something black and bigger than I can look at creeps out of me into the toilet. I flush it away with my shit. I cry all night. I take two sleeping pills. The next day I don't get out of bed.

Adam returns. His landlord wants us out in a week. He's selling the place. Adam keeps his distance from me. He's cold and moody, as expected. I find us a new flat, borrow my dad's clapped-out pick-up and load it with the nonsense we cart around to fill our lives. We move. I've given up on the screenplay, on lectures. I can't find the will to walk that path again. I have no money to pay rent. I take my CV to the restaurant downstairs but I don't turn up for the shift.

I interview for a job at the leisure centre. It seems as exciting as plucking pubic hairs from a toilet floor with a pair of tweezers.

I am one of fifty contenders. None of us want to be here and yet here we all are, blinking at the stone, cold walls in a vacuous stupor, competing for a role that will slowly tap our blood away. Do any of us remember getting out of bed, putting our clothes on? How did we manage it? Am I even wearing any clothes? I am ushered into a room with a group of nine dysphoric anaemics. Under the interrogation of no less than seven judges we play out their team test. Brainstorming. We're all understimulated and undersexed. Our professional masquerade is a farce, as stormy as a squeaking fart. A girl with a tangerine face mask won't let anyone slip a word in edgeways. I ask if anyone else has ideas and the flabbergasted muskrats all blink at me gormlessly. Well don't look at me. I don't have ideas. I'm waiting for inspiration to climb through the window, knock me out cold and drag me away from this country. Without a word I stand up and march out the room.

Rain falls, plunders the homeless, and floods the city. We're all thrashing in the sewers. Adam has taken to unrobing models in the living room to expand his artistic portfolio. I stay in bed. Most days I stay in bed. I'm not even grateful for having one. I start puking again, and before I'm through I gouge the pus out my face with my fingernails. If only I could gouge out two hundred millennia of evil and finally be done with it. I lose sight of where I am and just keep going. Infection banquets on my face. It spreads like leprosy. I keep at it for months. When our mates come round I won't see them. I can't bare to go to college. I decide to give up on the film. I'll never please them anyway.

One evening Amy is around. She is a cute actress whom Adam always urged me to cast in my films. I didn't think much of her acting talent but I took his advice as if he knew better. No. I took his advice to make him happy, as if that would therefore make me happy. I can't reveal my jealousy so I crawl out of bed to join them in the living room. As I open the door I hear her say "It would hurt her." She's in her underwear, sprawled out on the floor, propped up on her elbow. Adam turns to me, camera in hand. He wears his don't-mess-with-me jaw. I feel like a ghost in the doorway.

"Sorry to disturb."

I know how the rest of the conversation went. I shut the door behind me and go back to bed. I spend days planning which bridge I'm going to jump off. I play it all in my head, every street I'll walk to get there. "Go," I keep telling myself. "Move," but I can't get out of bed. I've spent hours fantasizing about hanging myself in the shower, or climbing to the top floor and launching myself down the stairwell. But I couldn't be sure it would finish it. The bridge was more fool-proof. But I can't move my legs. I hate myself for being too lazy or cowardly to make it end.

Endless nights bleed into endless days. The world is a gangrenous wound. Nothing ends and nothing begins. Nightmares gas out my room, choking the ether from floor to ceiling. No colour is this shade of pathetic. They're rotting me out. The stench of decay is so fecund that I'm gagging. Dad calls and tells me I have to sort myself out and get a job. I hang up and turn my phone off. Maybe I could strip. Adam comes in and says he's being evicted. He's overstayed his visa by eight months by some freak accident only a stoner is capable of. He starts to cry. I follow him into the living room. He's crouched on his knees in the far shadow of the corner, wailing. I realise he's hyperventilating. I find a paper bag he can breathe into and cup the back of his head. His breathing slows down and gradually smooths out. He gives me the weight of his head. It rests on my chest. His tears run like children.

"I can't go back there. I can't go. I hate my country. I hate my family. I'd rather die Laila. I want to die. I can't."

He asks me to go with him; he describes the Cape Cod coast, consistent waves. I could surf again. We both could flesh out and freckle, come back to life under the sun, dine by the ocean, walk hand-in-hand and have conversations like real humans, glow with good dreams and wrestle in the sand dunes. Hell, we could even adopt a dog. He knows all my soft spots. He pulls me into him, his eyes widen to the size of spaceships. He says,

"I don't want to leave you. I don't want to be without you."

He kisses me and we shoot off six million millennia of sexual frustrations there and then on the sofa.

"I've been saying I need to get out of this hell hole since I got here."

So I agree to escape.

In one night I write a new film, a joke. I have to turn something in to get my certification, a pretend pass to a pretend world, but one that may con all the con artists. Then again it might not. We shoot the film. It's awful. Adam takes over the directing and I find myself edged onto the sidelines. I feel like I'm watching this happen to me. I can barely move through my fog. Where have I gone? I feel like a puppet. I tell myself it doesn't matter. I have a way out of this life. I'm going to America.

7.

I am sitting on a high-rise balcony in Amsterdam. The shadows of a tree slide across the school beneath me. I've been watching this shadow play for hours. I've been high since I got here and I haven't eaten in two days. Adam took an earlier flight and waited for me here. I cleaned out the flat and sold his belongings. A man is hanging out his underwear on the neighbouring balcony. He has a rollie between his lips and headphones big as doughnuts. He dances as he moves, a rhythmic jerk, like a velociraptor.

Adam is reluctant to do anything besides comparing cannabis strains in coffee shops. We walk with our cameras, wandering a lattice of bridges and canals. He leads me to the scarlet streets where girls flaunt their wares behind windows. They used to honour them in temples, when prostitution was sacred. I feel unexpectedly vacant. In the flickering lights the girls don't look human but like puppets on a stage, some tangled in their strings. I stop and make eye contact. A girl stares back at me, flutters her fake butterfly lashes. Tears attack me from nowhere. I feel like a missing poster of myself, only there is no face inside the image. I wipe away the tears. She saw them. He doesn't.

This morning I went out alone and rented us a moped. I sped us out of the city. We found a windmill. I felt his smile kiss my back. But the promise of intimacy died before it kindled. He lies supine in a single bed in the corner. He is staring at the ceiling. He has his pegs on and his ice pack. Nothing seems to unplug his face from the pressure of the interminable migraine. My own bed furrows into the other wall. I watch the clouds clump together like pieces of a jigsaw. Raindrops ping off the railing and hit my nose. The raptor's underwear will get soaked. I could climb over and save them but it doesn't feel appropriate. My tummy's turning somersaults. I check my phone. Fifty minutes since we ate the mushrooms. They should be kicking in soon. I want to stay here in the rain. The room's thick with his pain. I'm cold. The rain falls heavily now. The writing in my journal blobs together and drips off the page. I roll it into a mushy ball and throw it over the railing. I aim for the gutter. I miss.

I traipse inside and lie down on my bed, mimicking Adam's dead soldier position. He doesn't speak so I don't. I'm feeling a bit panicky about the mushrooms. Maybe they were a bad idea after another hunger strike. I ate mushrooms before on a boat off Sumbawa. We rowed the dingy to the land and I climbed trees like a monkey. Adam threw his serving up. The walls seem to be leaning towards me, as if the room wasn't small enough.

For an unquantifiable eternity I lie in paralysis as I lay impotent for all those flaccid weeks of my suicidal inertia. The room convulses. Every edge falls towards me. A hundred thousand faces flash before my closed eyes. I don't know any of them but I know all of them. I can't breathe. This was all a huge mistake.

My life was one big mistake. I ruined it. I need to get out, to go back. There's no home to go to. There's no exit and no entry. I'm not supposed to be here. I can't breathe. I want to be dead. At some stage, I remember Adam standing over me.

"Are you okay Laila? Laila?"

He's there but I can't reach him and neither do I want to. I'm not safe with him. He's a monster or my lover. I don't know which. It's not safe. I try to run and to speak but I can't and this petrifies me. I'm choking. I'm asleep but I'm awake. I try and I try to wake up. I can't wake up. Make it stop. Make it stop. Turn it off. Adam's shaking me, talking to me. Now I can't hear him. A voice speaks over him. A male voice, loud and clear and bass, resounding from another place, muting out my reality. He sounds older, wiser, infinitely wiser. Infinite. I don't remember his exact words.

"You mean like the matrix?"

"I want to leave now. I made too many mistakes."

"Go to America. Tell him you love him."

Then he was light, a figure standing before me glowing white, emanating through me, through the room. He was gone. I knew with a certainty I'd never known before to trust him with my life. I knew him like I'd always known him. He was of another place. I can see Adam now. I can hear him.

"Did you hear that?"

"What?"

"Was I talking?"

"You were mumbling, groaning. Your eyes turned back inside your head."

"I love you."

He hugs me.

"I love you too."

8.

Sober. Ellis Island. They're all prancing in kilts and dancing Strip the Willow. For three days I've been followed by twenty bagpipe players honking out the same dismal song. I want to ram their pipes up their assholes. My national anthem. I've been waiting to escape Scotland for two years. I've travelled nearly four thousand miles to be greeted by a circus of my national identity. This is a nightmare. A stout New Jerseyite with a Scottish surname and a shiny forehead is piloting the launch of a new tartan to commemorate his clan and every immigrant Scot who crossed the Atlantic to start a new life in America. Over a roasted pig and a prized single malt he recounts with full-bodied pride his tribe's annual march on the Scottish capital in the full regalia of their tartan.

"We amass the biggest clan and beat the loudest drum."

He's beat it at me all weekend. Frankly, it stinks. We smile and we listen. There's no space to edge a word in if I had one to edge. My anonymity scolds my throat, or maybe it's the drambuie that is burning my language to ashes. In the bosom of his ancestral pride I feel as Scottish as his German Shepherds do. I belong to the world, if it'll have me. Will it? I used to think so.

Adam is being paid to document this charade. I am not being paid to assist him. I have aborted my role. I am imitating a funambulist on some layabout girders I have found in a stowaway nook of the island. It is as far from the pipers as I can get without swimming.

The steel is too thick to solicit my focus or adrenaline so I sit down and spark another cigarette. A fat seagull lands on the railing. Yonder she is surging from the sea in all her splendour. The goddess of liberty seems to mock me. I journey backwards in search of a time when I have felt less at odds with anyone. The gull is giving me the beady eye. I unpeel my orange and lay it out for him. I can't bring myself to

swallow. Apparently neither can he. He squawks and flies away. I open my book. "The Republic". I can't end a sentence without forgetting where it started. I need some water. I need to get my hands on some weed. In ancient Rome she was worshipped by emancipated slaves. In Notre Dame she unseated the Virgin Mary and announced the age of reason. "To philosophy." When will I stop feeling sorry for myself? What the fuck am I doing here? What have I done with my life? I want to dive into the ocean and keep swimming. The worst that could happen is she won't swallow me whole.

Light spills through the wall crack and bathes the holes in the bedframe. An overturned fireguard bows to the light spill. Layers of peeling paint crumble into chalk dust and swirl above the floorboards like ghosts. The walls whisper all the stories of the immigrants who left behind their homelands and journeyed here with their life in a suitcase. They poured in like a flood. Some married here on the island to gain entry. The forgotten died of famine or dysentery or diseases, locked in quarantine. Some gave birth in these tumble down buildings. Some were born. Who will I be?

Norman, a museum guide with the air of a ghost hunter, leads me through the hospital wing, piercing the black with the blinding headlight strapped to his helmet. These renegade buildings drift in the fog of the forgotten, refusing to leave behind the time that breathed life through them. They still exhale it. I love dilapidated spaces as I love watching flowers die. Where does the dust go? The disintegration brings me comfort. We are not supposed to be here. The Health and Safety Federation haven't yet had their way with it. Norman tells me he has worked happily in the Ellis Island Museum for 40 years. When he takes off his name badge, he steps beyond the cordoned barriers, glossy cabinets and tourists photographing their cheesy grins with cameras on sticks. Now a man with no name, he slides through a crack in the wall and slips down the spiral staircase to a maze of unlit corridors exhaling memories. We step into a damp room.

Stalactites drip from the ceiling. In the corner a cube of pull-out drawers reminds me of my mother's filing cabinets.
"Welcome to the mortuary."
He announces this with a wild grin and his childlike fibre of indestructible passion. We walk to the ruins of the special inquiry hearing room, where I presume thousands were interrogated for crimes they did and didn't commit. I feel guilty just standing here. An old, familiar poison creeps through me like a nascent disease. It sucks the air away. Does Norman feel it? I don't think so. I'm not Yahya Jammeh. I'm not Pinochet. Sometimes I feel like I am. Do I want to play the movie of my life as a checkout girl or the Sundance Kid? Am I a murderer? Norman is smiling. I breathe in the silence. The scratches on the wall are written in an Italian that I don't understand. I see a loopy flourish and translate it as a love note.

The bedroom is thick with potpourri, the smell of dogs, and velvet upholstery. We have been put up by clan Currie on an anonymous street in New Jersey. Adam is sleeping or pretending to. He has his ice pack on. I stare into the long, skinny mirror. I went too far again. My spine is poking out of me. Would I fail the island's immigrant medical checks and be turned away again? Probably. I wouldn't fail their drug tests. I've been clean for four days now. At the airport they led me to an interrogation room and searched my bag and my body for two hours. I don't have an onward flight and I wear just the right face of wanton, innocuous naivety to suggest I would be duped into acting as a drug mule. They found nothing. I'm choking the void with hard tobacco. It's 6 a.m. Oh God. Another day. The hours drag by like a fat pony with laminitis. I climb in the shower. When I return to the room Adam is not there.

He sits at the breakfast table spooning cheerios into a beard that is so bushy now I've forgotten the contours of his face. I wish I could grow a beard to hide behind. Maybe I'll buy a burka. I wish I had a dick or a tail or some wings. I am lacking appendages. The family sits around the table. Susan, our boss's wife, is towering over them, serving out pancakes and buttering Adam's with stories of her triumphs on Wall Street, in case he wasn't listening the first three times. He wasn't. Rob is forking sausages to the dogs. I can't bare to take the empty chair in case she inflicts the royal wedding memorabilia on me again.

She notices me behind her.
"Oh Laila, you're here. I managed to acquire you an apple."
I feel my cheeks flame crimson. Every head turns to me. I can't face eye contact. I'm so hungry I feel sick.

"Thank you Susan. I'm just going to take a walk."

The streets greet me with the hostility that oozed through her words. The sun scolds my forehead with vengeance. I have a headache. The tarmac bubbles. Everything feels sticky. "Special needs" is how she put it when I said I'm vegetarian. Over the table she glared at me with slitty eyes that said, "So you think you're better than us?" I've seen those eyes before. Was it my mother? I'm an invidious, ungrateful guest. I can't just take what I'm given.

The bus rolls through strip malls. Every second car is a 4x4. They look like overfed ants. I lean over Adam to look out the window. Utility pole after utility pole. He has his pegs on and his ice pack. I prefer his silence to his moaning. He hates the bus. He hates New York. He hates the journey. He hates America. Except for the pizza. He didn't eat pizza. We didn't visit New York. I wanted us to rent a flat there. He hates me.

We stop at a service station. I'm thinking, "Finally I'll get some food." He is whining about his migraine and the billboards and the sunshine. I'll never drag him to the beach. I can't bare to buy food. I buy more cigarettes instead.

The bus rolls on. Why didn't my ancestors leave Scotland? Were they cowardly? Were they backwards? Did the circumference of the village tuck the world into their belt straps? Maybe it's something I'm missing. Roots. Thank God Mum had an affair and got me out of there. Otherwise I'd probably have married a boy down the road and knocked up four kids by now. Kids. I could have. I start to squirm in the hard seat that's doing my back in. I feel the tears shoring up again. I open my book. Of all the books, why did I bring the fucking Republic?

"Adam?"

"What?"

He's annoyed that I've disturbed him.

"Do you have a book with you?"

"In my bag. Big pocket."

I rummage in his bag. It's so neat in there. Camera cleaning kit. Contact lens solution. Cheese puffs. Cookies. Topless woman tilting out a glossy pink magazine cover cupping her plentiful tits. Book. I turn it over. "Catch 22".

Fine. Let's see if the words don't fall off the page.

We disembark in Boston. People ebb and flow in all directions like marble patterns in motion. Adam leads me past the pretzel stands, ice cream carts, and burger diners to the local terminal. I hate being led. It's his country I suppose. He speaks to a man dressed in blue and marches back towards the bags that I'm sitting on. I watch his clenched fists and the rickety right leg that starts to bow like a sail when he's angered or tired or underfed.

"There's no bus until 4 p.m."

"What time is it?"

"10 a.m. This is a fucking joke."

"We could put the bags in a locker and go explore Boston."

"I was at college here for three years. I don't need to explore it."

"But I wasn't."

"No. It's way too much hassle. We haven't slept."

"I'm okay."

"I'm not."

"So we wait."

"I feel like shit."

He unzips his bag and takes another extra strength Excedrin.

Those things give me a headache.

"There's nowhere to fucking sit."

"Yeh. Six hours here is a really long time."

"Fine. Where are the lockers?"

We ride the tube. He leads me to a park. The sky is spiraled like tie-dye. We watch the swans weave around the empty boats while he reminisces on the ex-lovers he once brought here. Athena, Aphrodite, Daphne, with different names. This, of course, is titillating me. I'd throw Adam in the lake and fuck them all. If they were here.

His mother greets us at the roadside. She gives me one of those wholly American hugs that makes me feel like cookie dough. She's like a little Bluetit in my arms, all bones and feathers. She has a Persian composure, Adam's Bambi brown eyes and hair the color of ravens. She was an air hostess in the glamour of the '60s, now a nurse. She could have been a model. She still could be. She shares my mother's name. I find this confusing.

We bundle into the monster 4x4. She asks us about the trip and Adam's ongoing headaches. I'm falling asleep in the backseat and thankful for the excuse to stop speaking. I recognise all the town names on the big motorway signposts. They're all coastal towns in England. I have the sensation of having been here before. The telegraph wires slice the clear sky into geometric fragments without meaning. It's all too much for me. A hawk glides overhead.

"You've stopped taking Prozac? Does Dad know?"

"I feel better without them."

"But the migraines?"

"I had them anyway."

I let my eyes close and I sleep.

The sea air croons me back to consciousness. My eyes are full of sleep. Adam's window is wide open. He hangs out of it burping air. The cool breeze washes over my face, rinsing off the past and the journey. Horses graze in a field beside a cemetery. The crucifix gravestones are as white as shells, like the picket fences and shingles of the houses. The town appears to have washed up from the sea.

"He's keeping himself busy with golf except he's injured his knee. He's on the town committee, you know?"

"No."

"Oh yes, he's very active in local politics. We hosted the last meeting at the house. I baked meatloaf and carrot cake and they scoffed the lot."

I don't know where we are but it feels like we're arriving. I have that feeling I get on the last strait of a long journey. I've been begging it to end since the beginning. Now I don't want to arrive. I don't want to move. I want the world to keep moving me. I want the salty air and sherbet houses to rock me forever in this blissful, cocoon between waking and dreaming. I am nuzzling on the bosom of the open road. Not having to make a choice is the greatest freedom I know.

"Laila. You're awake!"

Fuck.

"Sorry, I dozed off."

"We're nearly there"

"It's so serene."

"This is Chatham."

In the dusky onset of evening, the peaky woods on either side of the smooth, hilly road glow a deep, luminous teal that I want to bite into. The indigos in the shadows are so rich it hurts. My eyes are lost in them. Adam pulls his head in.

"They've turned the old schoolhouse into an ice cream shop!"

"Oh, that was donkeys ago, Adam."

"I didn't know."

We pass Deer Meadow and Echo Hill, Stillwater Pond and Lovers Lake, Moonpenny Lane and Windsong Landing. I laugh out loud when I see the sign for Knob Road and a huge phallus looms over everything. 'Knobhead' was my brother's favourite epithet.

"Why are you laughing?"

"Oh, nothing."

My local village was woven of Spylaw Road, Abbot Seat, Butcher's Street, Hunter's Bridge, and Horsemarket. What does this say about me and my ancestry, or about our relationship with place, each other, and ourselves? I rack my brains for romantic compensation. Mayfield is the best memory I can conjure. That was the road to the garden centre and the shallow riverbank beneath the towering chicken wire fence where Dad, Kev, and I sat in anoraks with our fish suppers, feeding greasy chips to the ducks.

I feel the sea before I see her hot-pink ripples echoing the sunset. "Welcome," she whispers as the car bunny hops the smooth, undulating road named Shore Bay. By the time we arrive, the water is midnight blue. Corridors of tiny lanterns light the driveway. The house ahead is a looming shadow of shapes that I can't decipher.

"Dad bought the Wilky Waves plaque for our anniversary." Adam's mum says.

A light pings on above a door. I see it is the palace of the coastline. Frank greets us at the doorway, spreads his arms wide and gives me the grand tour of his dream. He is shorter than me, balding and skinny-legged but his aura extends across the ocean. I notice he shares Adam's bow legs. He introduces every corridor and cabinet like a great conductor teasing out the movements of a symphony. Every book, vase, cupboard and decanter, every reflection of light has its proper place here. Maybe it's the spaces between them. The oil paintings sing beneath fixture lights. The designer grand piano glows like a steaming, black stallion. Through the wall-to-wall windows I can just make out the squiggly reflections of the now jet-black ocean. She seems to rise right up to the house. I never had an interest for interiors. They're stuffy and obnoxious. It's nature's design I care for, but I can't deny he has created a masterpiece. He reminds me of my mother. They share the same birthday. Do I believe the stars shape us? I could make connections between anything; an uncle and a hat stand, a porcupine and a door knob. I realize I have drifted from his oration of the history and acquisition of the grandfather clock. I haven't a clue what he's told me.

"Laila!"

Adam is sailing my bag up the wide, winding staircase.

"I'll take it Adam."

"It's fine. Come with me."

He leads me to the furthest of five ensuite guest bedrooms. It smells like fresh paint and cedarwood. Two single beds hug the walls at either end of the long, boat-like room. The spherical windows look like portholes. Red, white and blue duvets are printed with yachts. In stark contrast to the house, it seems intended for children. Grandchildren. Thank God they don't know about the abortion.

"Lets camp out here. It's less pretentious. Thank fuck he's not flying an American flag like the neighbours. American fucking pride. It's gross. It literally makes me gag."

"Sure. I like this room. It's like a boat. I need a cigarette."

"Come on. Let's go outside."

He guides the way with a flashlight. The garden is a mystery of shadows I can't use memories to decrypt. We climb a mound towards two white sun-loungers facing the sea under a blossoming tree. He brought a whiskey. I think I hear an owl toot. Maybe it's my fatigue.

The wind is cold and keeps me awake. The stars are bright and clustering. When did I last look at the stars? The wind howls. The branches rustle. Beneath it all I can just hear the sea lap. In the distance, the beam of a lighthouse slowly swivels. I search for the moon and find its crescent behind the swaying branches. My numb hands fumble in my pockets. Empty.

"Can I borrow your lighter?"

He passes it to me. Our hands touch for two beats too long.

"She asked about us. She doesn't understand that we're not in a relationship."

"What did you tell her?"

"I told her I don't care about you like I cared for Stephanie. I mean I didn't know it then, but now I think maybe I loved her."

I have a lump in my throat that's suffocating me. My body aches. I repel it.

"She asked why I brought you."

"What did you say?"

"You're my best friend."

"Do you still speak to Stephanie?"

"No. She left for Holland. Then she went silent. I think she was angry. She waited. She wanted me to tell her not to go."

"Why didn't you?"

"I didn't know how I felt."

"Then it was too late."

"She was just a cool chick. She was so cool. And she saw me, you know? She showed me how to let my guard down and open up to her."

"Can I use your lighter again?"

He places it on the chair arm. I light another cigarette. My drags are long. The burn feels like a friend. He journeys down a corridor of ghosts, goddesses they sound like. As he tells his tale they each sound more alive than I am.

"In the end I just felt numb and empty, with all of them. It's like a defect."

"Maybe there's nothing wrong with you. Maybe they just weren't the right girls."

"Yeh. I don't think so."

"One day you'll find her and fall in love."

I wrap the jacket he lent me tight around my knees.

"I'll never love. It's how I am. It won't change."

"It's so good to be away from the city, to see the stars."

"Dad has a crazy, big telescope."

"Would he let us use it?"

"For sure."

"I've never looked through a telescope."

"No way."

"Way. Never. I'm pretty cold."

"Yeh? Let's go inside."

I'm wondering what the hell I am doing here. In the single bed by the door I'm in too much pain to sleep. I feel my body eating itself up. The wind howls against the porthole. I soak in my regret, pickling in it, wondering if I should just tear away into the night. He snores loudly in the opposite corner, the duvet over his face. As soon as the sun peaks, I dress and tear off running. I aim for the lighthouse and climb down to the beach. The wind is still swirling. It carries the sand, pulling it this way and that, shaping a new world like a child with a spade and a bucket. Its whirlwind stings at my cheeks and my ankles. The sky is blood red. Minute by minute the blood drips off its page. It leaves the coldness of steel. Its metal twirls with pools of frothy milk that overflow the sky and churn my stomach into knots.

The beach seems deserted. Here and there seagulls squawk viciously in a battle over crab's legs. One looks up as I pass with dripping, purple innards dangling from his beak. I feel so weak pushing against the gale I wonder if I might be going backwards. There's no landmark to chart my whereabouts, only a skinny spit of sand sandwiched by sea that seems to stretch into eternity. An arch of gnarled driftwood claws out of the sand. It looks like the locked jaw of a Triceratops. That'll do. That's a landmark.

I find several of these twisted, flotsam signposts. A raven's claw, an octopus, Michaelangelo with a peg-leg, a hunchbacked sailor staring at his toes. The music in my headphones shrieks like the emaciated anger that fuels me. I don't know what else powers my hamstrings that now accelerate like a cheetah. This energy is not of me. It rises out of the sand. I don't want to turn around. I never want to turn around. I'll run on until everything has vanished. Except what the hell is that smell? It smells like death, like sumo wrestlers burning.

I round the jagged curve of the landform and nearly stumble over the hulking heap of sea lions dozing on the wet sand. I say heap because some are sleeping on top of each other. They seem to stretch on for a mile. Not one of them reacts to my arrival. I can't be very interesting. The smell is obscene. I have to hold my breath. I turn around. The wind is behind me, but running back is always more painful.

Back in the house, Evan and I move down to the basement. Its enormous cinema is broken up by pillars, antique furniture and framed news cuttings that chart Frank's stairway to fame. Moptops and bellbottoms grace Tinseltown lawns. Even the mullet can't hide the glamour of his journey. Adam inflates a double mattress and throws it in the corner that hugs the door to the toilet. He hooks up his Playstation to the projector and plays Halo on the big screen all night and all day. The surround sound speakers blast me with grenades. Large trophies and Adam's accolades line the shelves. Adam in ice hockey kit, Adam in heat. He told me many times he was a child prodigy that would have gone pro if it wasn't for his body's adamant refusal to beef up. One of the headlines reads "National U.S. Player of the Year." I pick it up.

"Hey," I say, "what's this?"

"Oh Dad made it. It's not real."

In fact, I don't know whether to believe him. His conceited egotism and reticent modesty have always been somehow perplexingly intertwined. This room has "favourite child" written all over it. Maybe I wrote it. I feel jealous.

On the wall beside the big silver screen two framed black and white photos catch my attention. One is of a man's feet on a cobbled path. The other is of a bicycle and two longing women propped against a crumbling barn.

"Are these yours?"

"Dad took me to Italy."

"I like them."

He springs up and sashays to the door beneath the stairs.

"Come on."

The storeroom is sprawling. Big containers line the shelves with stowaway secrets. A drum kit sparkles in the centre of the Acropolis. He jumps on the stool and starts thrashing.

I have nothing to lean against. I stand awkwardly with too many feet. I feel like I've never done anything worthwhile in my life. His drumstick snaps, pings up and hits me in the face. His beat grinds to a weird halt.

"Are you okay?"

"Yeh. It didn't hurt."

It did.

"I wonder if I have spares."

He saunters around the shelves, pulls down a box, yanks off the lid and rummages inside. Ice hockey pads fly out, an enormous remote control helicopter.

"Nope."

He pulls down another box.

"I think this is it."

He lovingly lifts out an old pentax, opens a large, manilla envelope and leaves through a stack of grainy, black and white photographs. He looks through them slowly, allowing each its time to seep in. Memories inject through his body, inhabiting it with softness, hardness. He wears it on his shoulders. I stand over the box and look down. Camus, Chomsky, Huxley. Seneca. He said he doesn't read.

"Can I borrow a book?"

He holds out the photos. He knows they will move me. I take them. They do.

"I spent days in the college darkroom. I skipped class. The tutor would make a hairy deal of it in front of the others but after he'd say, "You know I salute you. I had to do that." He was like a father, I guess."

In his art is the Adam I'm always searching for, the hills and pathways that whisper, "You're not alone here," the gazes that tear through your heart. There are friends, smiles, girls, soul, and beauty. He saw in them what he's never seen in me. Where are my friends?

Where are my memories? I feel I have none.

9.

A few weeks after arriving in the US, I get a job at a sandwich deli on Main Street. I wake at 5:30 a.m. and walk there through the half-light. I pass the beat-up corvettes in the derelict gas station. My boss is called Michelle. She is sun-kissed and crinkly. She seems tired but full of vigor. She speaks like a cassette on fast-forward with a strong Boston twang. Maybe it's the caffeine. She is either much older than she looks or much younger. It's hard to tell.

I prepare sixteen vats of coffee. Different roasts. The smell speaks of times far away: Sufi mystics in Yemen, Ottoman envoys on donkeys, African slaves singing into their lunch leaves on sunkissed plantationsinCuba.Beforetheshiftisthroughmyearsareblockedwith submarine buns and I am squirming for oxygen in my cling wrap of grease.

The day ended at lunchtime when my soul was carted away on the juice truck. These recycled hours of the afternoon are stolen from my future in the vestibule of hell. Another girl rings my orders through the till. She shows me how to spread butter. They must think I just emerged from a Palaeolithic vault. Michelle pilots our every move. Portioning is her pastime. My dollops of hummus and coronation chicken are either too big or too small. I can never conform to her NASA calibrated quantum gauge that isn't anywhere to be seen except her scowl. She thinks I'm an idiot.

In the subterranean storerooms she shows me where to find napkins and root beer, mayonnaise and pepper. I've already atrophied to the size of the margarine squares, as if I've been turning rancid here for a decade in the comatose monotony of the plastic yellow chairs and the emergency alarm. Her orders are endless. Re-stack the fridges. Clean the dishes. Polish the tables. Replenish the coffee. I want to ram her face in the till drawer, if she'd give me a key, which she won't. I see my future before me. One day, probably tomorrow, my brain will implode. I'll drift down here and climb inside the deep-freeze to stare into the eyes of the salmon and snuff out.

The days pour silently through the hourglass of time; weeks leave my life, traceless as voles scurrying soundlessly beneath me. I go to work. I run. I sleep. Adam plays Halo. Frank stoops down to the cellar on nightly visits to announce which Hollywood producer he's forwarded Adam's CV to. Frank shot his way to the penthouse suites of a leading LA production house. I get a strong impression he will do whatever it takes to steer his only son down this path of fame and fortune. Naturally, he just wants him to be happy.

"Thanks."

Adam doesn't look away from his game. Frank sits down beside him.

"What are you playing?"

"Halo Four."

"How are the headaches?"

"Oh you know, the same, as always."

I leave Frank's unrequited yearning to bond with his only prodigal successor and go outside to smoke a cigarette. The stars look too far away to think about. It hurts my brain. I feel them through my body, so they're as close as my own heartbeat. But even my thoughts feel beyond me, drifting over the milky way. The icy wind bites my face. My skin is blue again. I got down to eating only one pickle at lunchtime. Now I've stopped binning the free lunch. I only take it to appear sane and avoid questions. I eat it on the walk home and puke when I get in. Then I run, as far as the spit stretches before it's swallowed by the sea.

On one of Adam's highs, I echo Frank's suggestion that we move to New York. He hates it.

We don't watch films anymore, except the three blockbusters Adam plays on repeat. He won't watch foreign films. He hates subtitles. I once persuaded him to watch "Stalker" with me and that was the end of it. I've stopped suggesting we visit the surf beaches or a gallery, live music, ice hockey or any event that would require him to drag his sorry ass out of the basement and live. He'll only say he hates the air, or the sun or the country. He drives to Boston to pick up weed. I give him all my wages. I start receiving emails from my lecturers about completing my coursework. My mitigating circumstances are expiring.

Where the hell am I? I open the documents and close them again. I can't even write my name. I think of all my grades and commendations, the scholarships and praises and prizes for excellence. The more praise I received, the more I needed.

"It was good, Laila. It was great, Laila. I read your thesis, Laila. It was spellbinding. Outstanding. Inspired. Astonishing. We've created an award just to tribute your contribution. They're quoting you in a book and you're only an undergraduate. Stay and do your PhD. I simply must be your mentor."

What a lot of drivel.

"I'm going travelling."

I remember seeing promise in myself, everyone and everything, a beauty like the sun that shone through all the fractures. That was someone else. She wasn't me.

The old patterns possess me. I become obsessed with the idea that my teeth are falling out. Everywhere I turn I see day-glow whiteteeth. When people speak I'm not listening. All their words are drowned by my unrelenting inner dialogue on their dental hygiene, which always points to the conclusion that I'm evil and fucked by the devil. I start gouging my face again. It starts with picking a zit until it bleeds and then squeezing all the pus out with the need to extinguish the impurity in me. I try to flatten them but end up creating craters, which pus and scab. In the mirror my teeth are orange and rotting. My clothes no longer fit me. I hide myself in Adam's sweatpants and hoodies. Frank looks at me like I've crawled off the streets, started squatting in his mansion and shitting all over the carpets.

Under extenuating circumstances for mental health reasons, I'm trying to finish my film school course from a distance. Adam says he'll write my overdue essays for me. I don't argue. I know he won't. He finds an old bottle of adderall pills in his boxes and deals me out a portion. Over a month of all-night stints, I write the essays. I steal one or two hour naps. Perhaps I never sleep. Who knows anymore, what's sleeping and what's dreaming and what's real? The days overlap and never finish. I edit the film and lay the sound on. It oozes like the biggest lie I've ever told. One day, when I die perhaps, I might eventually wake up.

The chatter in the kitchen rises over me like tidal waves. So many voices wanting to be heard. Adam's sisters, aunts and uncles are staying over for Thanksgiving. The kitchen is a battleground. I need to eat so I can puke. I ran eighteen miles. I've waited four hours. I can't wait any longer. Can't they all just fuck off? I'm such a self-serving, obsessive-compulsive, socially-defective bitch. Too many bodies between me and the fridge. I need to fucking eat. I'm a pawn on a chessboard trying to plot a path to the queen. Frank leans his back against the marble counter, chest puffed out, hands-on-hips, legs spread-eagled. Jeopardy. This is his signature pose. I spy him from the door. His body expands, claiming its territory, declaring, "This is mine. I invite you all before me."

Neil, Adam's brother-in-law, leans his back against the island counter opposite. In retort he lounges into a deeper slouch of liberal relaxation. He is gulping down the vintage red and weaving verbal dressage around the latest speech of the Republican primary. A red alert sign sounds in his wife, Anya's, ears as she eyes them from the fireplace. We all hear their cavalry sharpening their spears and warming up their horses.

I make a dash for the fridge and find a yoghurt, some chopped melon. I don't deserve it. It's not mine. I'm a disgrace. What am I doing here? Eating all their food, ruining their son's life. I need to get out of here. Where will I go? Everything's fucked.

"Laila."

"Hi."

Shaking, I look up from the melon I'm spooning into a bowl. Elizabeth is smiling. My heart thumps a hundred beats a minute. My eyes are wide as saucers. My eyelashes flutter uncontrollably as I mumble and look away.

"How are you?"

"Really well. What are you making? You always make such interesting creations."

My face overheats. I'm going to combust.

"Fruit. Sorry. Excuse me."

I slip out of the back door and storm into the night. I'm sprinting away from the house with no idea where I'm going. I'm running away. Rain swirls the world into running colours and liquid slush. I dart past the lighthouse and over the suspension bridge. My body feels like a sack of broken glass. The roads are slop. My mind is spinning a loop the size of a needle-eye. "Disgusting, embarrassing, failure, bitch." An approaching, black, four-wheeler blinds me in its headlights.

Everything's so loud. Its tires fling an icy puddle up my neck. It spits across my face.

"Bring it on!" I scream, welcoming the hate it spews across my life. I laugh uncontrollably, a laugh that cracks through the sky and jerks into the ear-chilling cry of a gargoyle. I terrify myself. I'm going to jump under the next one. I hear an engine purring louder and poison my legs with the intention. Spring, spring fast into the headlights. I see her face behind the wheel, poised and full of purpose, wishes and scars and fingerprints of the people who care for her. Spring, bitch. But she slows down and passes by me with her face made of clay. I missed my chance. There'll be another. There's always the dressing gown rope and the chandelier.

It suddenly occurs to me that I'm limping. Pain is shooting up my buttock like the kind of needles you'd use to tranquilize an antelope. My wet clothes cling to me. The sky sinks blacker. The pain is going to snap me. Where am I going? I have to walk. I'll book a flight away from here. I'll kill myself alone where no one can be hurt from it. A car stops in front of me. A man steps out. Oh good, maybe he'll rape and kill me and save me the hassle. His shadow rushes towards me. Hopefully he'll kill me first. "Laila" He hugs me.

"I've been driving around trying to find you for hours. We've been so worried."

He's crying. I'm crying. I feel like I've just woken up.

"Adam. I don't know where I am."

I see her then, split off from me, staring back at me, whispering soothingly in her tormenting way,

"I'll see you again soon."

I start fainting. The first time I smack my head on the cold, concrete steps. Adam carries me inside. He's kneeling over me when I come round again. He tells me his mother is worried. My flesh is hanging off my bones and I look like a skeleton wearing someone else's skin. She says she won't let me go home like that. She feels responsible. I tell her she's not. She won't hear it. They drive me to see a therapist. The man says he can treat my cannabis addiction but no more than that, then he asks me to pay him $150 for sitting in his chair and listening to my own tripe.

Adam goes on tour with a musician, documenting seas of screaming teenage girls from Illinois to Denver. Outside concert halls they punch each other to reach the railing and touch his ass or get their tits signed. The job was arranged by Frank, lovingly, through a highly revered contact. Duty-bound and waging a war with a world plotting to control him, Adam calls me over the internet from every hotel stop. With ice pack and pegs on, he lies on crisp, insipid beds, offloading his migraines, a travel-sick life in a mobile prison and the futility of his existence in a myopic country pioneering a soulless world where everyone is hating everybody and poisoning the atmosphere. His calls are the only hope I have, someone to share my own revulsion and hypocrisy. We rile each other into a vengeful, bloodthirsty spree in which we sadistically dismember everyone from the federal cabinet to the family kitchen and any other scallywag we can find to blame for our own foibles.

I move upstairs to the powder pink guest room where vintage dolls watch over me from antique, glass cupboards. I hate those prim dolls with their snub, judgmental faces. Twice a day I defile them with obscenities as I charge into the bathroom to vomit. I spit the same abuse at the mirror. I try to read the books from the pile on the chair but I can't see the words. Everything is blank with my aching to be dead. I promise myself I would do it, if Adam and his parents' false idea of responsibility for me were not my responsibility. So I add them to my hate-list for keeping me alive and to their faces I thank them every day for supporting my existence.

Adam returns. For two days he showers me with the affection of a Sufi mystic in rapture. He tries to seduce me in the shower. I can't feel my body and I cry. He drives to Boston to buy more weed and his love lilts into vapour. I find another psychotherapist. Our first meeting gives me hope. Unlike the last four she didn't say she couldn't help me. She doesn't seem remotely shocked by my confessions. She always says, "What if we look for the good in it?"

What if we did? I've never met a human so stoic.

All day Adam sits in the windowless basement and plays Halo with the lights out. Every evening, Frank staggers down the stairs and festoons us with an emphatic, no holds barred speech on Adam's brilliance which only serves to annoy, patronise and disempower him. I smile and wag my head like a car nodding dog, backing up Frank while wishing he'd fuck off. Meanwhile Adam tightens his pegs and doesn't turn away from the aliens he's blasting to entrails, offering no remote semblance of listening. I have to quit work before I make a stroganoff of the boss and fashion a bomb in the cafe kitchen that will light up the Cape Cod coastline. I'm disgusted by my own paralysis.

One early morning, beneath the wedge of the moon, I am trudging to the cafe past the battered corvettes in the disused gas station. I am wondering if they'd still move, if the engines could summon that cryptic spark of life, if I could find out how to hot-wire on the internet and run away with one, or if I should just clamber inside the giant box labelled ICE. An owl twits overhead but I don't see her. A siren flashes in the road. I step towards the dazzling light like a drunk at a disco. My body's running on empty, spinning like a Catherine wheel in euphoric, giddy spirals. I'm enraptured and vertiginous with the forgotten sensation time was always out of grasp and I may have felt this dazed for just one second or all my life. I see the moss green truck blocking the whole road, an italic, brown scribble and an acorn down its side. The forest warden is standing in the moonlit street with a silhouette, like Jesus Christ the Saviour, legs together, arms spread, faceless in the darkness. I follow the arch of his neck towards a hedgehog shuffling gallantly down the middle of the road, without apparent concern for foxes or weasels or being flattened. The saviour steers him onto the sidewalk. My heart fills with courage. I walk into the deli, deliver my notice and that is the end of that.

The next week I'm electrified by a less placid siren. Of course, my cataclysmic wakeup could have happened anywhere. But here it all looks so devilishly chaste and immaculate, a postcard resort town, manicured, sullied only by me. The rest seems pure as sea shells, fake as Disneyland, flushed with the scent of salty, ocean air, freshly mowed lawns and candy shops. I only notice my anarchy reaching its apex in such a place now that I'm running from a police car with two burly men at my heels, wondering how exactly it got to this. I blur past a mockery of white picket fences, paths of white pebbles and mailboxes painted in plush, pastel, ice-cream shades. Hand-painted plaques announcing 'apple tree house,' 'ocean breeze,' and 'barn owl cottage'; children sell lemonade and men trim hedgerows; blue jays and cardinals hop in the treetops and rainbows of hydrangea bloom everywhere.

The air is dense as fruit loaf and pregnant with everything I crave, but I'm scared I don't belong to. It's all rising like a film-set in the unbearable furnace of the midday sun while my feet slap the pavement pathetically. I've never run so slowly, now I'm running for my life. What was all the idiotic training for? Ten million miles for the grace of a penguin.

The man running at my heels demanded at the checkout that I open my bag and show him its contents. I knew in the aisle that everything was amiss but I was too drugged by my ritual to believe it. I've finally been hoodwinked by my own insanity. Perhaps I was ready for the consequences and had always been begging for the ending, but when the shit hit the fan I felt anything but ready. Comatose, I stared blankly past the checkout man and legged it.

Now, it's too late to go back and say, "Sorry about that." I'm wondering if I could deviate from the highway and find an elk corpse to hide in, some way of thwarting the inevitable. No. I'll just run and keep tugging up these ten tonne sweat pants falling off me. When Anya and Frank find out, I'm fucked.

The sirens scream past me. I can't breathe. I feel like my heart is trying to shoot out my throat. The screech of the handbrake-turn pierces the sound barrier. Three officers leap out in concert. They're as choreographed as dancers, except they're armed with massive assault weapons and standing firm as a concrete wall.

"Alright. It's over."

I stop dead and watch the world spin away from me. I leave my body, sucked up by a quantum leap and a force I'm too petrified or anaesthetized to contemplate. I look down on a girl I recognise but don't know. She hands over the bag. "I'm sorry," she says. "I'm so sorry" and she meant it. She meant it more than she could ever contain. Nothing matters now. There's nothing left to control. I'll be locked away as a maniac, despised by all I know, and yet I've never felt so safe or so free. A warm breath wraps around me, white and soft as wings. "Thank you," I say, knowing full well that I'm home.

The three policemen drive me back to the ocean mansion. I'm shaking uncontrollably. By some grace I can't fathom, they hold me in a cradle of innocence I haven't known in all my life. They tell me they are concerned for my wellbeing and want to speak to Adam. I find him in the dark basement playing Halo. I explain the stealing, the puking and the day's dramatic turn of events to him in a delirious sentence. He had no idea of the life I've been leading. Without a moment's hesitation he leaves to talk to the policemen. I sway in the basement, drunk and seeing stars, weeping uncontrollably. I feel like I've just woken up from the strangest dream.

"You've been leading a double life."

"Yes."

He comes to me and holds me. I shake and weep in his arms.

"I'm so sorry Adam. I'm so sorry."

"Shhh. Shhh. It's okay. It's going to be okay."

In the evening I ask Adam's mother if I can talk to her. I thought my confession about the stealing, the eating disorder, and the suicidal thoughts would be the hardest thing I'd ever have to do. I was wrong. The hardest thing was my silence all these years. She holds me with a forgiveness I never dreamed that I deserved and tells me she was once bulimic too. On the day my darkest secrets were uncovered I've felt more real love than I have in all my life.

10.

The Boston skyline is smoky grey and eerie. A skunk roams the garden beneath us. We are staying with Adam's sister and her husband. Adam hates them both. He stares at his phone for the third time this minute. We are waiting for a call from our dealer. We've been waiting for two days now. He's out of town. I am puking my guts into a bucket. The contents are liquid green. I woke at dawn and ran along the sea for two and half hours. There's no food in me. I took a photograph in the mirror and saw for the first time that my skin is hanging off my bones like leathery chicken flesh. My hair is flat and limp. My tits are non-existent. Guilt weighs on me. The guilt of looking like a prisoner of a death camp and knowing I am the only prison guard in here. The guilt is constant. It's all I know.

I haven't made myself sick since my ride with the police. I caved in to Dr. Belkin's persuasions to give antidepressants another go. I have reached the point of having nothing left to lose. My friends have vanished. I've lost them all. I told my family not to contact me. I am nobody. I don't even have ghosts.

I wake from dreams while still in them. I wake paralysed and suffocated. A shadowy figure hovers over my bed with her hands squeezed around my neck. I can't move. I can't breathe. I know I'm dreaming, but I can't wake myself. I try to call out for help, but I can't speak. I teeter in the terror of a life I can't die to or live to. I'm terrified of falling back to sleep, so I sit on the veranda and stare at the stars until it's light enough to run around the ocean.

I puke more bile when I go back inside. My body is rejecting the pills. My brain hammers against my skull. Can't stop. I do my sixty sit-ups, sixty press-ups. I'm thinking it's not so bad. In the old days it was five hundred a night and fifteen flat-out sprints up and down the stairs. I tried to hide them, to make it look like I was fetching something. If I didn't complete every last one of them my thoughts threatened to pulverise me and told me not to ask dangerous questions.

I faint on my way to the corner store. I wake with my head in a fence on the edge of the pavement. The pumpkins on the doorsteps are all grinning at me. I decide it best not to tell anyone. I realize I might die any day now and nothing matters to me anymore anyway. A swallow sails over my head. I smile.

An old man is sitting on a wooden chair inside the door of the corner store. He holds an old, knobbly walking stick between his legs. There's some kind of animal engraved on the top. Maybe an eagle or a hawk. His jaw moves in his face as if the screws have come out their hinges.

The store is tiny. They're playing reggae. Two young guys in shell suits and white snickers throw plastic-wrapped bread and bottled milkshakes on the counter. Behind them, a woman in a tight, grey pencil skirt holds two baked bean tins and breaded chicken fingers. She's on the phone. I wait behind them empty-handed. I feel something sharp poking my leg. His stick. He clears his gruff throat. His voice is so deep and bass it rings out on the streets.

"Eat something girl. Eat. For Christ's sake, eat!"

The woman on the phone pauses mid-sentence. My cheeks flare red. Everyone in the store stares at me, waiting for a response. I buy a hard pack of cigarettes and light one at the door.

Dr. Belkin wants me hospitalised. It is complicated. I don't have healthcare. I've overstayed my visa. Nothing petrifies me more. Adam says he'll come into my next appointment. When he offers to protect me, I love him and I shrink. I am feeble and helpless. That's who I am now. He's still giving me advice on inner peace in tireless, hyper monologues about his own mental victories. He takes to the character of caregiver with unrestrained excitement. It's my only path to affection. I know this, but I've walked so far down it I'm lost.

It's my fourth appointment. Adam is paying for them. I feel so guilty for his charity. It's greasy. Dr. Belkin tells me the gift's been offered to me, I didn't ask for it, that I have nothing to feel guilty for. I still feel guilty. She knows he's coming. When he marches into the room, she recoils and nearly drops her clipboard. She wavers on the spot like a deer in the path of a tiger. She hugs her notebook to her chest, smiles and invites him to sit. I feel it then, the power of his energy. I thought she was as steady as a rock, but he's got all his weapons out. He has flick knives. He's juggling them in the chair. I haven't seen him like this for a while. In the same instant I feel repulsed and protected. I don't know if I love him or hate him. He tells her that the hospital is not financially possible. She says she'll look into it. He leaves the room. We breathe.

I stop taking the pills, but I'm still puking green acid. My skeleton is poking out of my skin. I can hear my body masticating itself. There's a hunger of the bones unlike any other hunger. I pass out again on the floor rug. Anya and Adam drive me to the hospital. My veins are tiny and parched and refuse to give blood. When the nurse finally catches one with a needle my eyes roll into my head, my mouth foams and I fall into an epileptic fit. This is my third. When I come round, they tell me I fell off the bed and my limbs sprang up like an electrocuted rodent.

On the bed in the white hospital room I sit with a thermometer in my mouth. The bright window is warm at my side. I hear birds chirping. I've never seen the sun look so peaceful. I realize I'm still alive. Anya and Adam stand over me.

We leave the hospital and end up in a pet store. It's agonizing to look at the parrots, but I can't bear not to. To have wings and not fly, to not know your home in the sky, to feel in your heart but forget in your cage what you were made and given life to do. Their colours are too rich for this concrete strip lot, where we tore down the forest and puffed out its life. One shrieks a grating discord and hops up and down as we walk past him. Another perches lifelessly on the roof of a doll's house, motionless like he's been stuffed.

Adam leads me towards the hamsters. I don't want to be implicit in this. I can't bear to repeat the past.

"I'm going to look around."

Tiny, furry litters of brothers and sisters yawn in nests of cotton wool. This place is a superstore. I half expect to see a zebra chained up in the corner. Instead I see a thousand or more snakes and palm sized pets imported and bred from all corners of the world. I forgot those exotic lands, the diversity of life, all the hunters and captives, the billions of born free and born caged heroes starring in their own personal journeys. I forgot all the newborns that don't know where they came from, torn from the breast and the taste of a mother's milk. They know only the world they wake into and the world they are fed.

Adam finds me with my eyeballs glued to a cage. To him I'm

just staring. He can't hear the conversation I'm having with the wondrous one-week old rat. His brothers are all sleeping, still pinkish, curled together inside their hut in a soft, patchy mound. This one's tiny, moist nose twitches pointedly, telling stories of adventure with his spiky, snow white whiskers. Moments earlier, he had hurtled towards me as I passed, begging to be heard. I wonder if the tanked fish swim back and forth their whole lives in search of the ocean. Did Broccoli Rob hear the call of his ancestors crying, "Come back?" Did he die without a home? How will this one die? Will he know what love is?

His big brother yawns and peeks out of the tiny plastic, red roofed orphanage, blinking wondrous eyes which see the world for the first time. Today's world at least. He eyes me hesitantly and scuffles out to nose my enormous nose through the cage between us. My heart backfires all around my body. He steals my rigidity and whisks me like egg whites.

We take them home. My moral stance on domestication collapsed in a moment of delirious love. If I am a wild woman, they will remain wild rats. Anya screams when we show her. She says they're filthy rodents that probably carry the plague and she won't step within a square yard of them. We buy an enormous rat house and set it up in the annex of the basement where Frank makes sporadic visits to his painting studio and we smoke joints in the hatch. Adam says Frank lost his sense of smell with the feeling in his right foot. He daubs clouds above his dusky oceans obliviously. In all likelihood he's getting passively stoned like the rats.

The first day they hide away in their little hut, a roofed shelter on the fourth floor of their temple. Mostly they sleep and yawn, cuddling head to tail like the twin tears of the yin yang. I watch the rise and fall of their tiny breasts. While they sleep, my heart breaks. Shivers surge through my body, a memory without a place, the sensation of slotting together with another like puzzle pieces shaped from the same clay. The most natural thing in the world. I cry in shock that I still can feel a connection.

11.

I dream of a little girl banging on the door. I've been refusing to let her in, telling her to piss off, but she keeps banging. When the racket's too much to bare, I wake from my dream, climb out of bed, and open the door. The little girl is me. It's as if time is turning backwards and I'm meeting myself, walking to greet me from the other direction.

I used to run away. They said I was running before I was old enough to crawl. The first time it was 1986. I'd just turned three. My parents sent me to school that year to keep me out of trouble and out of their hair. They couldn't buy a uniform small enough so I looked like an urchin in an undertaker suit. I lasted half a morning. The form tutor spied me trotting off into the woods at the end of first break. She yanked me from the sycamore trees and carried me to the tarmac courtyard where my classmates stood in orderly rows waiting for the order to move. Helicopter leaves fell through the sky. One landed in the teacher's hair. She didn't notice. The day was a succession of orders. I went home on the bus. The bus driver ran over a dog and we had to promise not to tell. The form tutor phoned my mother that evening and said "She kicks you know?"

My mother filled my wardrobe with designer, frilly dresses. I hid amongst their silks and tore them all down from the hangers. My brothers didn't have to wear dresses or look pretty or let anyone down for not being an ornament of sex. Mother said I was a wicked, ungrateful girl. The words wicked and girl were intertwined like wicker. They taught us that in Sunday school. Eve wasn't born a girl, she was born a woman. I thought God expected the same of me. But I had to sit at the children's table.

The nanny went ballistic over the dresses and beat me. I refused to get dressed, so she chased me round the room in my underpants. I had a nanny because Mum's father had just died. He had a heart attack on holiday in Germany and they said grandma had gone off the rails. They didn't say that the inexplicable ripper which attacked his heart skewered her heart too. The nanny was called Mrs. Grey, but she always wore white. Snowflake white like her dentures and her cotton-wool hair. I ripped the dresses off my dolls then I cut all their hair off. Mother ordered the hair massacre, since I never brushed my own hair. It hurts to brush my hair. My hair is curly and delicate as dandelions. Every time I saw Grandma, the first thing she would say was, "So you still don't know what a hairbrush is? Look at that rat's nest." I would say nothing but dream of setting alight to her head. Then mother would yank me up to the bedroom and attack my rat's nest with Gran's comb. "Hold still and stop being a baby." I tried to stop my tears from falling, but the tears just fell more.

They taught me it was wicked to cry like a baby and criminal to be mad, so when I felt angry or sad, I shut myself in my bedroom before they could send me there with no supper.

On Sunday afternoons we would visit Nana. At the adult's table they retold the church sermons over plates of roast beef and mashed turnip. Every so often my uncle burst into spasms of raucous laughter. Mother said he's ill and has to take pills. He wouldn't talk in sentences but he seemed more sane than all of them. My Nana's sister was actually her niece. Mother would say this is a secret. I kept so many secrets. Mother thought the tractor-man had a handsome, refined Scottish accent and I broke the bathroom mirror when I threw a shoe at Connor but Connor took the blame because mother wouldn't smack him.

We lived on the border between two countries. I lived in one and went to school in the other. My dad is Scottish and my mother is English. They said that makes me half one and half the other, but when the sports were on, I had to choose. I decided I was Scottish since we lived there. Mother sent me to elocution to diffuse my Scottish accent. This backfired since elocution became speech and drama and I venerated the drama with theatrics.

I woke early in the mornings when dad left to milk the cows. Through my big bedroom window, I watched the sun rise out of the earth. Most mornings a fox waited in the steading. They called it the steading because it was where the farmers who lived here before us kept their animals in pens. They had sheep and pigs and chickens; we only had milk cows. We had big sheds with concrete floors and metal doors. In the summer the cows grazed in the fields and the farmers drove the digger into the big shed to offload mountains of fresh shit. They covered it in black tarpaulin and weighed it down with tractor tyres. My brothers and I played chase on it, but Mother always said I mustn't because it made me smell like my uncle.

I searched for the fox in the woods but I never found her. We made dens in the trees and waged wars. Charlie was two years older than me. He hung dead rabbits from the treehouse to frighten me. I wasn't frightened, only saddened. I made mud bombs and threw them at him. He booby-trapped his bridge so I coudn't cross. I always fell in the ditch but crossed anyway.

In the garden I sat under the conifer trees and watched the crows swooping in from the fields. They tottered on the chimney pots, congregating for something. Once we made a scarecrow and I painted on a smile. But soon we didn't need the scarecrow because Dad had a machine that fired a bang like a gunshot. It frightened the cat. The sky was so big, I didn't know where it would end. I wondered if there were any girls across the sky who'd understand the way I felt.

There was a big oak tree behind the maths classroom. She hurled her acorns across the school drive in mutiny. Some days when I thought no one was looking, I wrapped my arms around her and felt loved after all. It's not that I didn't have any friends, but they made lists. I was often their second or third best friend one day and then they would drop me to fifth. Even second felt like a punishment. I would pretend I didn't care and tried to please them. That never really worked and probably never would. I tried to please myself and always chased the boys. The boys didn't make lists, or if they did, they didn't talk about them.

Charlie pissed the bed a lot. Afterwards, he would creep down the stairs and climb into Connor's bed, and then Connor would creep into my bed. I could smell Charlie's piss on him. Charlie slept in the attic. Maybe he was afraid because the ceiling was low and a ghost cat lived there. Sometimes I felt it clawing on me too, before it jumped out the window. The window could open by itself. You had to crawl down Charlie's stairs. They were only tall enough for doll people even though Charlie was a giant and not a friendly one. He smacked me in the face whenever he died in his computer games. The men that made Charlie's room up in the attic sang songs I didn't know. They were there for a long time. It seemed long because the leaves piled up in heaps that turned from red to yellow. Then they disappeared. Mum made fun of me for talking to the men. She called them the workers. I thought the workers must be a different kind of people I wasn't supposed to talk to. But I liked their songs and I missed them. I'd like to belong to other people. There was a girl beyond the field who I liked to talk to. She had tall legs and conker coloured hair; her mother said her name was Sarah. But she was the daughter of the dairyman who milked the cows and mother said they were common, not like us, and I was not supposed to talk to her. I think she probably was a lot like me. I was not like the "me" my mother thought I was at all. Maybe we'd be friends as close as sisters if I only got the chance to talk to her. Connor had nightmares and screamed in his sleep. His screaming frightened me because I didn't know where he was. I didn't know where anyone was except me and I didn't really know where I was at all. I liked how soft the cat's ears felt. When she was happy, she dribbled in my lap.

I don't remember when they started shouting. I think there was a time before, when I believed in love, but maybe that was only in a story. They would argue in the kitchen. Dad would still be wearing his boilersuit. Sometimes you can see things without looking.

I remember squeezing my head through the bars in the stair bannister. Twice I'd gotten it stuck but pulled it out again. Is my head growing? If she found me she'd tell me to go outside. But the sky was white and sad and outside looked lonely. A slither of light climbed up the stairs. It looked like a piece of a rainbow. Violet. Indigo. Blue. Green. Yellow. Orange. Red. When I held out my hand, it would float but it could not hold the sky and I could not put the rainbow in my pocket.

The yelling sounded like distant music when I wasn't listening to the words. Sometimes it got louder and then I could hear her throwing things and the plates were screaming on the floor. She would slam one door and he would slam another. Everyone was rattling in their hinges. The house was being beat up and they were beating each other, but nobody deserved it; when they smacked me, I knew I hadn't done anything wrong.

Often, Mum sounded like she was choking, like a sea lion in a trap. You could not hide from the echo. It landed in every room. Even in the dining room which I was not allowed to enter, but I opened the door to see if the echo got in there. Wherever I went, I could hear her begging to be saved. Sometimes I shut myself in the attic cupboards but still she drifted towards me. Who else could go to her? Who else was there?

I nudged open the door softly. I wanted it to know that I wanted to heal its pain, all the pain in the world. Did the door hurt or care? Did dad? She was sitting at the far end of the kitchen table, wailing into an empty, square box and a hill of sodden tissues. She looked at me like I'm a stranger. She looked like a stranger too, like some kind of animal with her puffy, half-open eyes and her blotchy face, raw as bruised chicken flesh. I sat beside her and said nothing. Her life story drowned the whole kitchen. I'd heard the story five hundred times. Every time the words bit deeper. Every sentence felt like an attack. They were like hungry sharks and I had nothing to feed them.

One day, she got tired of her story and said she can't do it anymore.

She said, "If I stay any longer I'll die. I have to leave Laila."

She made me promise not to tell anyone. I only told Miss Roberts, the gym teacher who was mean and scary and didn't like me much. After hockey, I locked myself in the toilet and all the girls were banging on the door. The caretaker had to break in. Miss Roberts ordered me upstairs. She said I couldn't leave until I told her. She said we'd stay all night if we had to. Dad would give me the silent treatment all week if I missed the bus and I couldn't think of a lie so I blurted it out. Miss Roberts smiled and said, "Look on the bright side. At least you'll get two Christmas presents." I cried more and said, "I'd rather have a mum."

She hadn't left yet. For months I carried what she said in my pocket like something dead but still beating. For moments I would forget and the world seemed the right way up, a land of love and equations that added up. For moments I thought, maybe she'll change her mind. But then I would come home to her wailing and the day fell off its axis again. Those days everything whirred into a distant haze; the kids unpeeling the plastic wrap from their sandwiches, playing tag on the rugby pitch, climbing into buses to go home to their families. It all seemed like a sick charade, a make-believe reality that had mocked me since birth.

12.

Mum did finally leave after a few months and stayed in a fixed caravan on Grandma's farm. She took Connor away. Charlie and I visited them every second weekend. In the mornings we ate hot buttered croissants with apricot jam and pain au chocolats. She called them our French treats. I felt guilty eating her treats. I'd rather she was at home and we didn't have treats. Connor was always laughing like he was on an exciting adventure. The caravan didn't move but I felt like it was travelling away from me at high speed. It had already gone five thousand miles. Everyone seemed younger. I felt old and faded.

As spring warmed into summer, we took the bikes out and cycled the hilly lanes in a landscape of corn, beet, and oil seed rape. The fields rippled like the sea, as our bicycles soared through their waves of yellow. I could hear the buzz of bumblebees all over that honeyed smell. Dad was with me that day, behind me. Sometimes I led and sometimes I followed. I pointed out the shapes in the clouds but not the rabbits in the hedgerows because he said there's too many and he would shoot them. Today the clouds looked like animal crackers, full of dinosaurs and peacocks. I liked to tell him about history, because he loved history and I was at the top of the class. We never talked about our history. I told him about the culling of the kulaks who had their land confiscated by Stalin. Most were shot or sent to labour camps or evicted to

Siberia, Kazakhstan or the Urals. I always thought the Urals sound like the urinals. That day I said it in class accidentally and everybody laughed. I liked to make people laugh; it was easier than being pretty. The boys called me pancake because I had no tits. They were all a year older than me because I started school when I was three. I didn't bleed, I had no hairs on my legs and I didn't wear a bum-bag filled with tampons like the other girls in class who flaunted them on their hips like they were walking a red carpet into the kingdom of sex.

The Urals are actually a mountain range full of semi-precious stones. I'd like to see them one day, although I expect they're still full of dead kulaks. Maybe all mountains breathe out the dead and that's what makes them feel so living. These hills talked to me like that. The fox still came to see me. I woke at 4:00 a.m. when Dad went out to milk the cows and she was there waiting in the steading between the dew and the shadows. We locked eyes and then she trotted away. When I would leave my widow open, the wind danced with my curtains. I left the window open often, so it danced on my skin. When it was frosty like that, I felt so alive.

Now the wind danced with Dad's hair and the spokes of his bicycle wheels. He looked more alive in the wind than I'd ever seen him, like a little boy. He wove his bike down the lane in bendy waves. When he looked at me, he was smiling but he had tears on his cheeks.

"Dad, are you crying?"

We shouted over the wind.

"No. It's the wind."

He swerved ahead of me and pointed his stocky finger at a rabbit that shot out in front of us and darted down a hole in the earth.

"Little bugger."

If he had his gun he would have shot her. The swallows were playing in the wind, dancing like kites, some doing backflips. The wind was singing and the hills receded in waves that faded to blue beyond my reach. I always thought the hills stretched into the future, like when you look at the stars.

"Imagine if the Tories took the farm away like Stalin."

"Well it's not quite like that."

"What do you mean?"

"Foreign import will take the farm away, because we can't make a profit."

"At least they won't shoot us."

Dad smiled his toothy smile that sometimes looked like a grimace.

Often I couldn't tell the difference. The clouds gathered in a halo shooting out sun sparks and columns of mist. The rain floated all around us, making my hair spiral into ringlets. A little corner of a rainbow climbed out of the earth.

We cycled over a small stone bridge. A brook trickled in the valley below us. There was a heron on the bank, waiting. Herons never look lonely, always where they are meant to be. The water sparkled in the misty light. The pebbles sounded like music. They slid together and smoothed each other into new shapes. It was like that with friendship sometimes. In the sheep field, the grass quivered and two trees leaned together like lovers. The sheep huddled underneath them. They had internal weathervanes. Some had white heads, some had black heads and one was black all over.

Sheep didn't have mirrors, only each other. Dad said that the next field was resting. The ruins of Hume Castle peeked into view on the hilltop. Wild geese glided over our heads and disappeared into the blinding light.

"Dad, are the highland cows female?"

"Yes. They'll have a bull inside."

"Why do the females have horns?"

"They have a pecking order. They fight for dominance."

"It sounds like school."

"You don't fight do you?"

"We don't have horns."

I've watched the bull when it was his time. I was one of the bodies that stands there waving my arms so the cows stayed in line. They shuffled towards the pen in a lazy row that stretches from the grass field with the ruin on the hill. They reminded me of sleepwalkers or zombies that moo, because they didn't seem to know why they were here and they didn't seem to care anymore. One at a time the workmen steered them into the pen. The bull's black, slimy penis lengthened like a telescopic umbrella and he went at them one after the other. The men laughed when I asked if he gets tired. They say he's had all year to rest for his big day. I'd rather be the bull than the cow. God, I was so glad I wasn't a cow. But I liked the highland cows. They looked so wild and free.

"Div!"

That's what I called him

"Can we go to the pond?"

"What pond?"

"The koi pond."

"Never heard of it."

"It's near."

I steered us onto the long stretch of road beneath a tunnel of trees that spindled up like towering witches. Dad took his hands off the handlebars and replaced them with his big feet. I tried to copy but I wobbled all over the road. The branches spilled across the sky like arteries. There was blood on the road. A big hare looked at me with bulging eyeballs. His guts dangled and sprawled around him. Must have been the crows. I shuddered at the thought of maggots breeding new maggots inside his carcass. The road fell into a steep downward hill. I raced the wind for momentum and glided on its wings.

"Laila!"

That's all I heard. His words were lost in the whistling wind.

"What?"

"Come back."

My heart raced in my rib cage. He sounded hurt. I gazed fleetingly at the fish and pedalled hard back up the hill.

At the summit he was gone. I tore back along the aspen tunnel. I couldn't find him anywhere. I returned to the hare. Then I heard a gruff voice calling my name out. Dad was hiding under a tree. He turned his bike away, and didn't even look at me.

"We're going this way".

I followed him. He's never cycled so fast. I couldn't catch up. I knew he was angry because it was written all over his back.

He would give me the silent treatment when he was angry. I knew this pattern. I had learned by now that the rhythm of his temperament was as dependable as the seasons. He was as steady as a rock until you crossed the line, then suddenly he roared with a ferocity that tore loose from the jaws of some wild beast on a distant continent. I was scared of that beast more than anything. I never knew where he kept it. After the eruption, he would plunge into a punishing silence that could last for days or weeks. Sitting on the same sofa, I'd try to speak but he'd block me out until his disappointment just boiled itself away.

So we cycled in silence as carbon grey clouds swept overhead and the hail came. Guilt soaked through me and I stung with the shame of not knowing what I'd done. I asked him later, when he'd broken his silence, "What did I do wrong on the bike ride?"

"Nothing. It wasn't you. The farmer with the pond's a bad man."

"Why?"

"Just don't go near there again."

I did go there again. I stood peering over the hedge, watching the fish weave amongst each other on their solitary journeys to nowhere. I found out later that Mum had an affair with the "bad man" and that's why Dad didn't want to be there.

Once a week after school Charlie and I would catch a bus from Berwick to see mum. The high school kids pointed and laughed at our private school blazers and threw biscuit crumbs at my hair. Mum said we should think ourselves lucky, they used to stick chewing gum in hers. A man would phone all the time. He had a posh English accent. He sounded embarrassed when I answered and stuttered.

"Can I speak to your mother?"

She's going to live with him, she would tell us. I didn't even know who he was.

Mum barged in once while I was in the bath. She never knocked. She looked at my naked body like I was filthy in a way that couldn't be cleaned.

"Do you know how to clean yourself down there?"

She gestured towards my privates.

"Yes."

"Have you started bleeding yet?"

"No."

"You'll be lucky if you never do. It'll ruin your life like it's ruined mine."

I sat in the flimsy bedroom staring at the acorns on the wallpaper, wondering how I'd find my way through this forest. It was 1995. I was almost twelve. That recent hit by Annie Lennox, "No More I Love Yous" was always playing on the radio.

"I used to have demons in my room at night. Desire, despair, desire. So many monsters."

I hated that fucking song.

13.

Sometimes he cries. I go in to say good night and he's watching T.V. in the cold living room. Tears stream down his face. He scoops them up with a firm, coarse hand, a farmer's hand, stiff as a shovel, pulsing with the earth like a tree root. Heavy legs and an empty wineglass rest on the low glass table-top. One red wine tear clings to the bottom.

"Are you okay dad?" I ask in half a whisper.

"Fine," he says, with a toothy smile and a thick Scottish accent that comes out more in the half-truths.

I give him a searching look.

"You know my eyes run when I'm tired."

The clock strikes twelve. I climb up the stairs carrying the weight of his grief on my shoulders. I shut the door on all I care for and sleep with the carcass of our yesterdays on top of me.

Charlie still lives in the attic. These days he doesn't venture out much. After school and at the weekends Dad and I drink beer and watch football on the living room T.V. We lie in the lamplight on the chunky burgundy sofa that Mum chose. It's Scotland, so most days it's raining. When I'm lost in reverie he pinches my knees which makes them rocket in the air and the cat shoots up like a missile.

She purrs while he strokes my calves softly. Our three hearts beat in rhythm. It's calm and warm here as we root for the same team. Even when they lose we're in it together. We drink and jeer with a belonging that I can't find in my church, my school or my country. It's more peaceful now without Mum here.

I used to take Dad's sandwiches out to the harvest fields. I'd climb onto a round bale and paint the hills and the castle ruins in the distance. He'd lift me into the combine harvester and I'd perch on the toolbox while we rolled up and down the lakes of dancing barley and sailed on the silence of our dreams. It was too loud to hear words over the rattling of the fan and I liked that. Our silent conversations were the ones I understood.

I journeyed with the wheat through the hungry teeth of the harvester, which stripped off my husk until I was nothing but dust floating off into the hills and vanishing. Then I ran through fields of stubble. Running, running, and running until I was the landscape itself and there was no mind left to take home with me. On dry days, the harvesters worked through the night, watched over by owls in a landscape without lights. Some nights I'd fall asleep on the toolbox. He'd cover me in his jacket under the spell of the moon.

When the bales were collected, my brothers and I would build fortresses with them. But that first summer after Mum left, Dad found an empty packet of cigarettes in the straw shed and banned us from there. I didn't visit the harvest fields. Dad worked later and later and we hardly spoke. I'd take the bicycle out and cycle the country lanes until my legs stung and my mind was as light as clouds floating in an endless indigo sky.

I started to skip dinner because there was nobody there to eat with. Kev took his to the T.V. and slammed the door shut. If I went in, he grunted about my ugliness, then told me to piss off.

In the school canteen I no longer joined the queue of hungry kids steering their empty trays towards the trinity of sphinx shaped dinner-ladies disguised with aprons and hairnets, serving up laden plates of battered fish and deep-fried chips, steak and kidney pie, and spaghetti.

Instead I entered my own hall, lit by buzzing fluorescent strip-lights and hidden glowworms, an enormous stark-white obelisk on the outer rim of heaven, where the other diners were mere holograms, as inconsequential as the salt and pepper shakers. I'd stare at my apple and cling-wrapped sandwiches as if they were porcupines that I had to wrestle down my throat. I'd scrape the cheddar cheese out of the middle of the bread and nibble around the crusts. Everything tasted of dust and cardboard, impossible to chew and like sandpaper to swallow. I shrunk to the size of a crumb. Soon I abandoned sandwiches for the salad plate. I ate the lettuce and cucumber and left the rest. Before long I just skipped going to lunch altogether and ran through the woods and walled gardens. The landscape shrieked into a kaleidoscopic dream: redcurrants and rosehips, foxgloves and bluebells, swirling in psychedelics that seeped through trigonometry and the French subjunctive and filled me full to bursting.

The world of school and family moved softly, like wispy clouds drifting in slow motion, as hushed as vestal virgins in dreamless sleep. I drifted into oblivion, where nothing and nobody could reach me, as if I had plunged into the musty pages of a gilt edged book and it had closed itself behind me. I felt so light, my feet walked on raindrops. After school I'd climb trees, throw down my shoes and watch them tumble to the soil that fell away underneath me. I'd stand on tiptoes on the tree's cool arms and spread mine out like she did. My feathers unruffled and stretched across my life.

I missed Connor. At that time, Mum and I spoke on the phone about once a fortnight. She'd moved to Essex to live with Michael, the machinery salesman with the polite, public school accent, a dead wife, and three children. Their fathers had been best friends since 1944, a bond they owed to Hitler. My granddad's farm served as a military base to the RAF towards the end of the war. Michael's father was a squadron leader based there after his time serving in Burma. He met Michael's mother in Rangoon. She lived like a princess with bed maids and a pet mongoose that slept in her sheets. It saved her from a snake. Of course I learnt that later. Now the fathers that spawned my mother and her new lover lay side-by-side six feet beneath the earth in a Northumberland churchyard. The fates of their first
children were intertwined in ways that I can never know.

She felt as much a stranger to me now as he did. A truth-telling letter about my anorexia from my friend's mother had gone down like so many of those spitfires. It crashed full throttle on the landing and went up in flames. My father's eyes blazed in the black cloud of the exhaust fire. We all needed somebody to blame.

Alana's parents had only wanted to voice their concern. I'd known Alana since I was three. We used to camp under the silky, queen duvet in her family's guest bedroom, feasting on foil wrapped chocolate liqueurs and playing pirates. We tickled each other's arms from shoulder to wrist, chatting until one of us fell asleep mid-sentence.

When we were older, I believed she was everything that I wanted to be. She took me to France to stay with family friends on an island off Cherbourg. She watched me push food around my plate as if I was conducting traffic. I'd lift my fork to my mouth, nibble at the edges of a haricot vert and return it to the plate. All I wanted to do was swim in the ocean, swim out to the indigo edge, and vanish. She had her period and my swimming made her angry. She laid on the sand amongst the nets of the fishing boats, her breasts dripping with the sun like ripe peaches on a tree after rainfall. They climbed out of her white bikini, beckoning all and sundry. We bought ice creams. I remember purposefully dropping mine off the sea wall and claiming it was an accident.

We hired rickety old bicycles and cycled across the island, discovering fort ruins frozen in time. Their crumbling windows looked like holes to another dimension, claimed by weeds and overgrown with lichen, a wall demolished to knee-height unable to die to its dead purpose, now standing between worlds and watching. All that really interested me was how many minutes I'd spent cycling. The rest was cataleptic. I was sleepwalking through catacombs, knowing my own coffin had been ransacked. Alana grew tired of me wanting to cycle everywhere. We got into an argument over apple-green syrup in a café veranda raised on stilts. Our battle jutted out into midnight blue abyss slashed with screams of flamingo pink and mandarin. The sky fell into the sea. I fell into the spectrally still inertia of the moon's reflection, drowning in our silence, wondering if in fact we were not upside down, suspended by physical laws that I never understood.

My arms were folded like crossbones, stinging with the bitter hatred of my triumph. I had rebuffed the sugar and protected my fortress. Alana stood up and left.

I floated towards the moon for hours, wondering what to do when the cafe closed and I was tossed into the night. At 2:00 a.m. I paid for the drinks and walked back towards the cottage. I left the bike. We had no lights. The road was wide, pitch-black, and deserted, undulating over an endless succession of hills bulging from the earth like corpses on a battlefield. Every stride stung through me like an infected laceration, and not just because I had to summon every ounce of my humility to stop myself walking the other way and finding a route to Alaska. My body wailed with exhaustion. I wondered if my body had always been screaming and I wondered how I had never heard it before. I staggered through the harrowing decibels, tripping over my feet, my fingernails squealing endlessly across the blackboard of the night. My knees were bloodied and dripping gravel. My face felt bitten by the acid of my tears.

Every ten or twenty minutes, blinding headlights would bounce over a hill and flame past me. I leaned in towards them with an analeptic lilt and swore I'd dive into the next light. Bright, cosy, firework lights. I tried. Four or five times, I tried. My head got halfway across the road and my feet wouldn't follow. When I reached the cottage I found it inert, swallowed down the gluttonous throat of the night. Relieved, I climbed the stairs and sank onto the mattress in silence. When I woke the next morning, Alana had already left.

I found her perched on a rock hugging her knees to her chest and trailing her silver ringed toes through the swirling eddies of the incoming tide. I scrunched across the bed of white clam shells to reach the protrusion of rocks and sat down on a slippery one amongst dozens of limpets. The icy ocean lip rolled over my legs and splashed across my lap. A shiny, black crab crept between us. We sat there in silence hooking unspoken words to fishing rods and casting them over the crashing foam into the lull of the sea. In the distance, a sailboat was gliding, smooth and voiceless as icing. My foot found hers beneath the water and they coiled together like swans.

After the letter, the screaming started up again. Only now I was in the firing line. At dinner I was no longer left to my own devices. Dad stood over me like a Sergeant Major and ordered me to eat. No threat would make me yield. I suppose it was the one thing I had control over. One day he strapped me to the chair with his belt. The same button hole he used when I was ten and couldn't or wouldn't consume all they served me. The difference between can't and won't was never very clear, especially when you're told what they mean to you. Charlie joined his team.

"You're an embarrassment," he screamed, as if I didn't know it.

"And you look like a freak."

I ran to the furthest corner of my room, where the peeling red flowers of the wallpaper could never protect me. I locked the door while Dad's fists pounded the inside wall of my brain, everything was trying to get in, to get out. Shrill, asphyxiating shrieks collided from every direction like trains without drivers, grating through my cell membranes with the squeals of striking metal twisting at speed. The corner opened its jaw and threatened to swallow me.

"Do it!"

It wouldn't. There was no hole to climb out of. I thought I would die with the pain, with the noise. Dad forced open the door and removed the lock. I lay face down on the bed, thrashing my fists. Eventually he went away and left me alone with the power of my own will. I saw that I could never stand up to it. I didn't stand a chance. It seemed

superhuman, indestructible. In comparison, my Dad's wild beast looked pathetic. It was the first time I'd seen the petrifying face of my own demon, seen myself in its clutches. Nothing in life is more terrifying than that.

When your body survives on its own flesh, you feel in need of nothing and nobody. I had joined a swimming club to feed my starvation. One night I was half way through the final set of ten 200m front crawl sprints when my heart stopped beating. I blacked out for a moment, came round and couldn't breathe. When I reached the wall, the coach told me to shower and call it a night. I was failing at everything except disappearing and that ached somewhere I couldn't reach, but more prominently, it felt like victory. In those moments when I felt most beaten and humiliated but too exhausted to care, I could feel the cold, upwards curve of an anarchist's grin like a nihilistic knife slash behind the numb mask of my face. I felt the beast gain an inch with every pound and muscle and friend that I lost. But she fed me more than food ever could. She was my beast and mine alone. She terrorized me, but she loved me, carrying me on her back as we hurtled towards the hot white subliminal edge where we were traceless. All I could see was a violent rush of colour and bright light, long shadows swelling towards me. How soothing that was compared to looking at the reality we'd created about us.

14.

The school bus releases a deep fart, grinding to a halt at the blue cottages at the bottom of the hill. Charlie and I climb out into the bruised, blue sky and walk the long, puddled road up towards the farmhouse. The fields are too marshy to wade through. Charlie stomps ahead of me, swinging his rucksack in his fist. The straps dangle into the puddles. I make no attempt to catch up. The dairyman's dog barks from the top of the hill, a Doberman, which once bit Connor's ass. The dog is on a chain but I still have pricks on my arm's hairs. The downy is thick now, white as snow, like an alpine forest, like fur.

Dad is sitting at the kitchen table wearing his reading glasses. He has a blunt paper knife in his hand. The handle is inlaid with wide, gold grooves. They nest his stocky fingers like a glove. He wears a stiff, blue plaster on his middle finger, so tight it must suffocate the blood flow. He said he caught the finger in the strimmer. The knife always reminds me of a crocodile.

Birds chirp in the trees as blue deepens to black. Charlie lifts a Ribena bottle from the top of a cupboard, pouring himself an inch, topping the glass with water before leaving to watch T.V. Rain tears at the window. It hasn't let up all week. BBC Radio 3 buzzes in hushed whispers from the corner under the window, gruff impassioned voices.

"Never say that the risk is negligible unless you are sure that your listeners share your own philosophy of life."

The day's post is spread across the oak table-top in neat piles; copies of "The Scotsman and The Scottish Express", a few hand-written envelopes, several bills addressed to David Rae & Partners, a letter for Mum and two pamphlets advertising women's clothes, which he has systematized in the pile furthest from him.

"Our knowledge of CJD goes back to earlier studies of kuru, the headhunter disease seen in Papua New Guinea, where people became infected after eating the human brains of their foes and preparing their dead relatives for burial."

He takes off his glasses and rubs his eyelids. I see his face scrawled with spidery, red veins that bleed across his eyeballs. He hands me a letter. It's from the school headmaster. I skim the page, racing for the end, trying not to fall in. The words "anorexia" and "medical attention" jump at me like piranhas. Then I fall in.

"We will of course welcome her back when she's fitter."

"I'm taking you to the doctor," he says. "Put your coat back on."

The car ploughs through the puddles, spraying jets like violent waves across my window. I refuse to look at him, tracing the moon as it follows us at each turn.

"Two of your friend's mothers have called me. They think you're dangerously thin. That was the word they used, 'dangerous.' They must think I can't look after you." The wheels are slipping on the road, under his grip. I plead with them to plough us into the fencepost.

"What have you been doing to cause this? Have you been taking drugs?"

He squeezes the words out his throat. They hit me like acid.

"No"

"What about medication? What are those antibiotics for?"

"For my skin Dad, for my spots. You know that."

"How many are you supposed to take?"

"One in the morning and one in the evening."

"Are you sure it's not just one? That sounds like too many. Are you taking too many?"

His voice skyrockets as he flings the wheels round a corner. Water splatters across the windscreen. I search through the sheets of rain for the stars, trying to remember, to envision the pill bottle's label.

"I don't know, I don't know." I was crying.

"What do you mean you don't know? Didn't you look? Don't you know how important it is to follow the instructions?"

"I'm sure it's two a day. I'm sure."

But now I wasn't sure at all.

I went in alone. A poster of a skeleton beamed down at me.

The doctor's flat, white hand guided me to the empty, plastic chair. Between us, on his desk, a purple human heart was skewered on a stick, throbbing with blue and red veins. A man with greying hair and a shiny bald patch typed into his computer with his back to me.

"How is your relationship with food?"

He spun in his chair and lurched towards me on its wheels. He smiled broadly. He had big, pink gums.

"Healthy," I sputtered. "My dad just misunderstood. I don't have a big appetite." He weighed me, measured me, did a sum on his calculator, and then pointed to a number on his wall chart.

"You're here," he said. I hid a crooked smile behind the solemn mask of my face. My demon was dancing maniacally in the icy waters of the blue zone as if I'd scored an A on a test.

"Ideally, we want you here." He pointed at the green zone.

"Okay" I said, smiling brightly and thinking, "Fuck green. I'm going to fall off the bottom of the chart."

He made me a referral to the dietician, called in my dad and said there was no sign of a problem and nothing for any of us to worry about. Dad's shoulders relaxed, dropping the weight of the Taj Mahal. It landed on my face. The two men shook hands at the door, laughing over a missed penalty at Easter Road, where Hibs play. My heart crawled under the floorboards. I felt shipwrecked, watching a rescue boat sail on by without stopping to pick me up.

Winter came. Snow fell and kissed every tree. The cattle were housed in the sheds, bedded until springtime. The outbreak of mad cow disease was tearing through the lands. It hadn't reached the herd, but it had poisoned the blood of Scottish farming and infected Dad's heart.

Snow lay like a coverlet across the deep, brown fields, and draped the hills in thick eiderdown, tipping their peaks like white chocolate. We skated on the puddles. I cracked them with my heels and watched the fractures swell like fractals underneath me.

The headmaster had allowed me to stay until the end of the school year with the hope that I might recover. I had just begun my GCSE requirements. He said it would be less disruptive to hold out.

Frost burst the drainpipes and school was closed for days. When the drains were replaced, we were four foot under snow and the school bus couldn't reach us. This was the silver lining of living on a farm in the middle of nowhere. Through those marooned weeks we slept over at Dad's parents and camped out with our cousins. Papa stood at the window in his tartan flat cap and slippers, spinning like a weather vane behind the glass of his binoculars while providing a lively commentary on the infinitesimal movements of the neighbouring farmers. In the sedative frosts of December, twitches of life were infrequent sights, like the scuttle of a field mouse skiing through the snow. We stayed up all night playing gin rummy. That was when I met Papa's beast. He rampaged through the conservatory poking his walking stick up to the heavens, begging God for our forgiveness. He hurled the cards up off the table into a tornado. We perched a pillow above the door so it landed on his head when he came in. He confiscated the card deck and made cousin Andy sleep in the bath.

Meanwhile, I was sleepwalking. At breakfast Nana would tell me, while cracking her boiled egg and buttering her toast, that she was rocking in her chair and silently knitting when I drifted past her and traipsed out into the snow. "I thought I saw a ghost," she used to say. I felt like a ghost.

I slept alone in the pink bedroom. The boys slept in the blue one. I listened to the wild laughter of their pillow fights beyond the wall while I was relegated to a powdery world of mirrors that mocked me. There were crystal decanters on the dressing table that my mind filled with poison, brass candleholders, lace doilies, and an eggshell pink vanity set embroidered with white and red roses encased in crackled glass. There was a hand mirror, a brush for your head and one for your dress, and a brush for who knows what else. I never touched them. They had that air my Mum sometimes wore, a cold exclamation declaring, "I'm only for decoration." Also, brushing my curls made me look like an electrocution victim and I was scared of a hairbrush. Mum used to yank them through my knots, cursing the infernal rat's nest growing from my head while ignoring the silent pleading of my scalp and calling me a baby for crying. I never saw the underside of the hand mirror. I was trapped without identity like the knitted dolls that covered the toilet rolls, screaming to scramble free of their woollen cage, dive down the plughole and find the sea. My eyes popped every one of the cream ceiling wallpaper bubbles before sleep took me. But I had books. Books saved me.

The ice didn't thaw. Snow kept falling. Dad drove us to midnight mass in the tractor-trailer. An apocalyptic flood couldn't keep us from church. Christmas was the hardest time, without Mum there. I got so cold that winter, my skin turned blue and plum purple. Now the downy on my arms was like bear fur. I liked those small consolations that gave me the impression I was achieving something. Everyone was trying and failing to make me eat. I drank so much water to fill me up Dad said it would make my head explode. Mum came up to stay with Gran over Easter. She said she was taking me away with her. I said she wasn't and she said it wasn't up to me. I stopped speaking to her. She gave me a day to pack my worldly belongings into a cardboard box. All I remember thinking is, "I won't get to say goodbye to anybody."

15.

Mum is reading a book titled "Stylish Napkins". "Drum and Bass" oscillates the room above, driving the ceiling towards us. She throws down the book and stomps out the room. I hear her feet punish the staircase, five steps and a hiatus.

"CHARLIE!!"

The beat goes on.

"CHARLIE!! Turn your music down. CHARLIE!!!"

The upstairs corridor creaks like a rickety bridge as she pounds her body along it, punishing it too. I think of a rhino stampeding. A door squeals open and music floods out like a dirty river. I see what she sees: a dark cave, Kev in the corner, stoned, hungover, hanging upside down from the day like a bat. The screaming match commences. Every other day I would tighten my grip on the brillo pad and scrub until my hands were raw and bleeding. I'd bend in near impossible ways under the counters to wipe the skirting boards clean of all this poison seeping through the ceiling and my cell walls. I'd devote myself to cleaning up this river, to making her happy. I'd be scared not to, scared of drowning in the rip current as she soups the deluge of our lives into the desert bowls and pours it over her own head and then mine to prove how much it stinks. But today a hummingbird is prodding its beak on the window above me. I desert my cleaning duties and slink out the back door into the sunshine.

My stepbrother turns from the soapy, cherished, white sports car that belonged to his late mother and soaks me with the hose.

"Bike-ride?" I ask with a mischievous grin.

We pull two bicycles out the mulberry bush that is climbing through the fence and whizz through the wooden gate into Suffolk's rolling grassland. A sharp left turn leads us along a narrow track through the pine forest where squirrels dart up the tall trees.

The smell of bark, cut grass and forget me nots swims through my nostrils and showers my organs with love, cleansing what the brillo pad was scratching into my bones. I've been forbidden to exercise. Rebellion sings in every cell of my body.

A dachshund gallops towards us, tongue swinging in circles, dancing with the air in delight. Sparkling pearls of sweat drip off him. Each one seems to be grinning in its oceanic reflection of sky and forest. Behind him, a man in a floppy, straw hat ambles along the path whistling. His eyes sparkle with the glee of his companion. I want to take them out his head and put them in my chest pocket.

We cycle over hill and country before reaching a flooded field where a swamp is trying to claim its home. We try to veer around the flood but miscalculate the terrain, pedal into its heart and sink up to our necks. With drenched clothes we drip home looking like bog creatures, where I am surprised to find that mum thinks the pair of us are a hysterical sight.

Mum and I walk along the rim of a ploughed field. Dandelions poke out the soil here and there. At the top of the hill an old windmill spins stories of our ancestors through the clouds. They bumble along in no hurry to get anywhere. A cockerel crows as if trying to start the day over again. It is the only time I can remember taking a walk alone with my mother. She is telling me about the nuns at the convent, about straight A's that became B's and C's when the syllabus was changed and a nun arrived who had boulders in her heart and the sting of a hornet. I watch the mud sinking underneath us, collecting on the whites of my trainers. Now she is telling me about her breakdown at university.

"Your dad wouldn't visit. All the other girls' boyfriends came at the weekends. Can you imagine how I felt? He was too afraid to ask Papa for time off. Do you know he wanted to join the navy but he had to leave school at fifteen to go home and milk the cows. Well I didn't really make any friends at university. There was Susan I suppose but I don't know if she was really a friend. We do still write to each other. Anyway, I was so miserable; the doctor prescribed antidepressants."

My heart hurts. Sometimes I try to close my ears but the sounds just get louder. Big globules of soil are tumbling down the muddy bank as we disturb their restful slumber. I think of the worms, plummeting in terror from their cliff face. Nothing can be saved.

"So grandpa drove down to collect me from Nottingham because he said no daughter of his would ever be medicated for depression. As if.....as if it was the biggest failure."

Her throat croaks. Tears stream down her blotchy cheeks as she talks about her dad's heart attack and the day her life ended. My shoes are heavy with mud, each footstep unbearable. My stomach growls like a black panther.

"Then all I wanted to do was have kids and Papa bought Dad the farm so we moved in. Well the farmhouse was a wreck and I had to decorate it with Nana who had such awful taste."

I am observing my footprints in the soil, disgusted with these ugly traces of myself I am still leaving behind me. I want to run back and erase everything.

"I finished my degree in Newcastle. On graduation day, Papa declared that agricultural economics was for academic idiots who knew nothing about farming. It was like a kick in the teeth. I gave up on my career and had kids."

The growling in my stomach is now hurting me. My panther is on a rampage, tearing through my insides, slashing up everything. I want to curl into a ball but I will never surrender. There is a suffocating stillness all around us. I am trapped on this path alone with my mother in the middle of nowhere and the whole world has stopped moving. I feel as if we were the last people alive. I beg the leaves to shake, a fire engine to arrive, the sky to stretch down and eat us.

Then she tells me about Jimmy, the farmer with the pond, the man who promised the world to her. He said he'd leave his wife, leave his kids. They were discovered. The gossip spread through the land like a wildfire.

"People talked behind my back. That's when I found out who my friends were and I'll tell you now Laila and save you the pain, never trust your friends. Everybody knew. Dad said he forgave me but he couldn't."

There is a path of pebbles that winds from my gran's stone farmhouse to the wrought iron gates that are painted black and smelted with vines that wind their way inwards and wrap around the word "PINEHALL." The gates are bookmarked by two pillars and watched over by doves. The path is fringed with big conifer trees. I zigzag between them, crouched above the burnt orange needles, collecting the huge fallen pinecones in my jumper for my grandmother. Little thrushes hop from branch to branch and crows 'caw' from thepeaks of the slender birch trees, creaking like old chairs in the woodland behind us.

There is a commotion at the conservatory. Adult bodies streak across the garden like phantoms and disappear into the woods. I set down the cones and creep after them. I can't find the path. I'm scrambling through a labyrinth of white trunks slashed with mouths.

They echo the adult's screams. The crows squawk towards the sun, which reaches through the woods with glowing orange fingers. They pick me up and pull me into the wildfire. Flames shriek across the corn, tearing up the earth, eating out the bales. I blink in an effort to comprehend this mania. Men sprint in all directions, yelling for water, my father amongst them, glowing red, shouting orders over the violent growling of the flames. He looks so limp and helpless, swallowed by orange tongues and black smoke, devoured by the burning fields of my mother's dead father.

After the flames die out the embers drift like a eulogy of black snowflakes across the lawn past the sun lounge windows. Beyond the glass, the family sit like strangers in a hospital waiting room, breathing in the starched tweed skirts of the great aunts and silently murdering each other. I try to enter but at the doorway I'm suffocated by the dirge of unspoken words and teacups chinking saucers. I go outside and lie under the weeping willow, unable to erase the recent image of my father now branded into my memory. I feel dizzy with the conclusion that he cannot protect me from everything and something has died in the flames.

He drives us home in silence. In the passenger seat Mum is a bomb that will detonate if we so much as move. Her thoughts drift towards me. Everything adds up to nothing. Connor lies in my lap and I stroke his soft, snow-white blonde hair, feeling an old suspicion worming its way through me. Nobody has a clue what they're doing. The trees streak past us too fast for me to hold. What kind of a world did we fall into?

In my new home in England mum's interminable Cliff Richard cassette is still playing on repeat. It's the same charade all over again. Her chicken flesh face and the vociferous wailing, porcelain in pieces all across the floor tiles. It's not my father, it's Michael, my step father, but the argument's the same. I refuse to eat her buttered toast so she locks me in my bedroom. My punishment is no school today. I expect most kids would see this as a marvellous gift, and those kids would be of the clear headed variety. But my head is full of horse shit. I freak out at the thought of missing a single advance of Operation Barbarossa or the jump of an electron. I might trail behind.

Mum used to say she was the pinnacle of the class so I suppose it became a sort of competition and an urgency to bridge the gulf between me and deserving. A "B" grade would mean my life was doomed to failure and the only thing left was to poke my eyeballs out with her knitting needles. Well, the needles were downstairs and I was trapped in here so I climbed out the window and ran through the fields until nobody's love seemed to matter.

All the same, battles over food continued. Meanwhile, Mum complained of having no money, then bought some feckless utensil or butter dish she might just hurl at the window. Her happiness seemed to lie in the next thing she could purchase, another crappy carrot cutter to distract her from the shade of the curtains that reminded her of last week. Half the days she festered into the folds of her bed sheets while wailing over her disembowelled wallet or the bulbous gash in her sports car that had appeared since she launched it into the gate after one of their louder disagreements. Those days she saw the glint in my eye that said, "I have no respect for you whatsoever." It's not that I didn't feel empathy, but that I felt it too much. I tried to cheer her up but she ricocheted every word and they crashed like numchucks into the mask of my face. In truth, she seemed only to perk up momentarily, when we let her loose on one of her tireless monologues about my father. But those speeches dragged on for toilet-flushed lifetimes I hadn't the patience or idiocy to endure. I told her I was through with it. She clobbered me in the face, yelping that the day I was born was the worst day of her life, then she ordered me to get out of her house. So I packed up a bag and at seventeen, I left for the world carrying the banner of freedom.

16.

On the third day, the rats build the courage to venture out of their cage. Balzac sits in my cupped hands shaking like a leaf. Blue is full of the moon, scurrying up my arms with excitement and wonder. He forages in my hair, making a nest of it, sniffing at my ears. His whiskers tickle. He climbs over my forehead to investigate my face. Fear surges through me like a rocket. I feel a sharp nip on my eyelid.

"OWWW," I wail.

Blue bit right through the blue vein that started to protrude when I was puking. He stares at me with big, sorry eyes, unsure what happened. I feel awful. I spooked him with my fear. I start to cry. He won't come out of the cage again. I stroke him, telling him I'm sorry. He huddles against the far corner with his back to me. Balzac darts out, scurrying up my sleeves and under my jumper. Blue won't move. He cowers in the cage looking lost and ashamed.

He haunts my dreams. I wake in the night with a leg in agony. It's my sciatic nerve. My stomach screams. I'm starving. It hurts to put my foot down. I have to hold the walls to walk down to the basement. The prospect of not being able to run today fills me with terror. My head spins with possibilities. What if I never run again? What if I never walk again? I feel like I've failed at everything. I treat my body like a dump house. Every worn out revolution of the turntable of my mind shoots poison through the nerve. It jets out my foot and my eyeballs.

The rats dart to the door to play with me. I forget about the pain and the running. Adam wakes at midday to find us rolling on the floor. He's wearing his pegs and a sour milk face.

"Hey."

"Hey."

He goes out to the hatch. I hear the whir of his weed vaporizer warming up. The rats scurry under my sweater. With my head on the floor, I watch him bang his fist on his chest and burp air. Deep, walrus belches. Where does the wind trap? Is it the same wind that carries the waves and dances the grass stalks? He cleans out his device with a bent coat hanger.

"How did you sleep?"

"Terrible, as always."

"Migraine?"

"The worst."

Tears start rolling down my cheeks.

"What's wrong?'"

"My leg. I can't run."

For the first time since this morning, I remember. I start to hyperventilate. The panic attack chokes me. He takes the rats and puts them back in the cage. He holds my back. I'm gasping for air. I can't find it.

"I have to get out. I have to go. I can't. There's no..." I scream.

"I can't breathe. I have to get air. I need air. There's no air. It's so dark. "

I limp to the hatch.

"Wait, I'll put my shoes on."

"I can't wait. I have to go. I'm sorry. I have to go."

I haul myself to the beach, dragging my leg behind me. My mind won't stop gutting me with new reasons why I ruined my life and my future's already fucked.

"Shouldn't be here. Shouldn't be here. Shouldn't be here." I have to shut it up. I want to concuss myself on the rocks. A dog is barking at me, leaping against his enclosure. A woman wearing a tall Russian hat and frock coat walks a poodle on the pavement across the road. They jerk like jagged shadow puppets fighting against the wind. I turn my head away. Maybe the whole town knows what happened with the police. I cut through a hedge onto the dunes. A snapped white picket fence sinks into the sand. The wind sounds like a woman trapped far away, but inside my own ears. I hear her suffering. I scream as I yank myself along.

"Shut up. Shut Up. SHUT UP!!!" I don't know if I'm screaming at the wind or at my mind. I long to comfort her. I drop to my knees. My leg hurts so much. I cry myself into oblivion. After an eternity I realise all I can hear is the wind. She seems to be crooning. I sit there for hours and just listen. Adam finds me and I stumble back to the house in his arms.

A gazelle tiptoes in candlelight. I hear Adam's breath. It slows and lengthens. The gazelle is Spanish. After the beach I downloaded a yoga class for Adam's migraines. At least, I tell myself it's for him. Self-trickery might bypass my bollards. We light our own candles and practice on the floor rug. The gazelle's class sit with their eyes closed as she whispers, "Exhale. Inhale. Feel the breath flow through your body." Her voice slips through me like maple syrup. With my leg pain there is little I can do. I breathe. Unlike my university days, the class is not steeped in thoughts of being inflexible, being bad at it or being bad in general. I don't have the energy. I'm empty. The ocean must have reached inside me and taken it all away. For the first time that I recognise, I feel my breath soothing me. I start to meditate every day.

Glorious days melt us like children. The past sparkles into star dust while we transform the basement into an epic rat city: an ambitious fairground of tunnels, hideouts, and flumes fashioned of boxes, toilet tubes, old shirt sleeves and driftwood. The rats take to it like children take to fairy tales, as we do. We teach them tricks and watch them grow, or they watch us grow.

Play, I learn, is the only true vessel of creativity. There I forget the rest—all the paralysing ideas of the cretin I thought I was, the conqueror I thought I wasn't, and the angel I must become. None of that gibberish matters when your loved ones turn flips in the air for the sheer thrill of it and dance for glee over a dinner of peas.

My pulse drums to the rapture of their tiny heartbeats as they dare to run faster, leap further, to fall and climb and somersault and falter, to fail and keep failing, to pick themselves up and never stop daring. As they build trust in me, I build it in myself. The trust to love and eat and play as they do. They race up my body and perch on my shoulders. They whisper in my ears. I dance them round the room. In these moments, euphoria washes over me and carries me to Eden.

I have to work with Blue to show him forgiveness. The eye incident scarred him for life. He is overweight and won't eat except in seclusion. His scar is the mark of a most beautiful sensitivity. I understand him more than I can show him. He is the artist and Balzac the warrior. In them I heal parts of myself.

The rats ripped my chest open and poured the world inside me. Perhaps the passage of our love is beyond the realm of words, like trying to explain music with the flourish of a feather. I can tell you that I fell through their world and found heaven; to give myself up to them was to forget I was human or woman or mentally ill—all the rhetoric I'd learnt to justify my experiences. The rats showed me that there was nothing to be fixed. In their mirror I was only the wholeness of nature I'd forgotten I was. To allow myself to receive love, to believe that I deserved that, was to wake up to life again and for blissful, unquantifiable days, to fall madly in love with myself.

Who would have thought that my greatest teachers and my doorway home would be so small to human vision, so powerfully beyond it and so thoroughly misunderstood? Perhaps I needed another creature who'd carried a plague, who'd been feared and maligned, to discover that a creature is not the plague that they carry and fear is the only real plague. In play and love, there are no judges, only total surrender to blurred ideas of goodness and evil.

Now this thirst is unquenchable, a thirst that fills me too full to talk about. I lie under trees and fall out of every box I ever drew myself. I fall out of words and clouds and whirlpools. Off canyons and mountains and star belts. Every living breath and being and heartbeat bursts through me: buds and feathers and pine cones and collar bones, fingers and lakes and toadstools and fish scales; everything there is, ever was, and ever will be—laughing, crying, and swaying as one inextricable entity. In these ocean hamlets my essence leaves my body and dances with the seagulls while the earth takes my flesh home, returning me to clay. For the first time, I remember feeling held by the world, by sky and by earth, cradled in an everlasting love without conditions.

The breeze dances my hair and all my stories swirl away like the sand dunes. In this is my only real memory: bliss. This body is my belonging as the earth is my body. My limbs are wind and sea and rock and sky. Sky is sky and a womb that feeds me breath, not a father I need to ask for forgiveness, no master stained with my blood. I kiss the ground and find my longing, the body that cradles the spark of my heartbeat, the end and the beginning, the circle wrapped around me like arms.

I start to wake before dawn, venturing out to the rocks to watch the day rise out of the sea. I swim myself full then sit on the rocks to dry, dangling my toes in the ripples. Three crows flap around me, landing at my side, then flying back to the chimney. Every day, a crow or gull joins me when I sit here. When ecstasy rushes through me from a sensation so simple and replete as the warm breeze kissing my face, a crow or raven swoops so close I feel her feathers touch my hair and her wings carry my heartbeat.

I spend the afternoons in the sanctuary of the village library and practice yoga in the evenings, upstairs and alone, melting into the maple syrup voice of the tiptoeing gazelle. I replace her with music. I dissolve into the notes, my bones, the vibrations of my cells. I feel them surge and sing and float and dance as I lie on the carpet and stretch into new shapes and out of old spaces. My mind lulls, floating on a silent song. I feel something happening. I have a body much larger than the body that I know. A home. A cocoon. A mother. She looks out of me. I look through her eyes.

I call on the crows from my bed and hear them croon back from the rooftop. They swoop over my shoulders as I cycle. In the garden they dart towards me from separate trees. Sometimes they do crazy things. One landed on my arm then somersaulted onto the phone wires. The hawks sail above me, spinning circles. A little robin hops on a stalk outside my window. He greets me every morning as I meditate. One day he brings his girlfriend. They sing me their duets.

Christmas comes and goes. At the pool I meet a lady named Robin. I'm standing there in the changing rooms with my top over my head and my tits out.

"I've never seen such a graceful swimmer in all my life."

I don't even bother to poke my head out.

"I'm less graceful on my feet."

"Well you were born for the water."

"Yes. I was."

I discover that she's an art teacher and an old friend of Anya and Frank. Before I reach the house, she's already called them. I'm told she's been invited round for cocktails at Frank and Anya's.

I hear her laughter over the gong of the grandfather clock. I can smell the formality from here. The maid girl with a pearl earring gazes at me in her unassuming way from a Vermeer anthology displayed on a chair in the hallway. It's funny how you catch glimpses of Frank's innocence just when you least expect to. Robin shoots to her feet when Adam and I enter the kitchen. She tells them all that I swim like a mermaid. Frank frowns at me. Robin cackles. She's drunk and babbling without stopping for air or reaction. I started tuning out while she was talking about Memphis. The men talk shop while pruning their feathers. Robin is twittering in my left ear about how her son has "the depression" and her husband "caught" it too.

Certain words just edge their way in there, like critters.

She makes it sound like the black death. I suppose it feels like that. Her perfume is suffocating me. I prick my ears to hear the conversation Adam is having with Robin's husband. The bastard's repeating everything I spouted in my whimsical morning euphoria. Word for word. I want to grow a horn right out of my forehead and skewer him to the wall. Instead I harmonize Robin's ridiculous mock laughter and cackle like an idiot. They weren't my ideas. I didn't write the Tao Te Ching or the Upanishads. He can have my words and shine his balls with them if it'll help him charm this high-shot film producer into giving him a job while I listen to the producer's drunk wife ramble on about shopping. No, fuck that.

"Tell me about your art." I say.

"Oh, I just gather driftwood and paint my little scenes on them. It's very simple really but people like them. They sell them up at the gallery."

"I'd like to see them. How did you get into art teaching?"

"Oh. Someone said, 'you could do that Robin' and I thought 'well, maybe I could.' " "Were you already an artist at that time?"

"Heavens no. I didn't have the confidence. Do you know, when I was in middle school, I could never get top grades. I couldn't even rise above C's. I had no confidence whatsoever. That started in primary school because the teaching was below par. I was bullied by those little bitches. Now the pretty, little girls come to me with tears in their eyes because I haven't given them an A. You know the type. They want straight A's and gold stars to show off to daddy. Well, on principle, I never give out an A. Nobody deserves an A. They can have a C or a B at best. I'm teaching them early that perfection is a mirage. Why feed their misapprehensions? There's no such thing as an A in life. There's only gullibility. They'll be stronger for it. Mark my words."

I catch Adam's eye. We make our excuses and leave. Robin has a message for me. I don't like it at all.

Adam and I make trips to Boston to stay at Adam's sister's house. His sister and her husband live in a Hispanic neighbourhood, where the painted picket houses chain down steep sloping streets. Adam and I sit on their balcony and plan films. We write scripts and start mapping out shots. In those moments, where Adam is most alive, I am in love with him again. We are lost in play, where I am most found.

Anya holds open the front door and leans into the sun. Her silk, blue night robe quivers softly and then billows.

"Frank. Frank. FRANK!!!! Come back in here this instant... FRANK!!! You can't roam around the garden with a gun. FRANK!! You'll scare the neighbours. What if someone sees you? Get in here or I'm calling the police. FRANK! I've warned you. I'm calling them now."

She grabs her skull in both hands and marches into the kitchen. He's at it again, hunched over the flowerbeds like Elmer Fudd, roaming with his rifle. Watching him I wonder if we all find something to blame for our anger. Frank has rabbits. I have Frank, Adam, my parents, my teachers, and the neighbours that plough through my meditations with their grass-cutters and hedge-trimmers and roaring garden power tools.

"Leave the leaves," my mind screams. The seagulls dive down and glide towards me. They soar over my head and sail on the wind. The seals swim over from the spit across the water where pastel, chalky houses sink into the sea. They turn somersaults at my feet and squeal out like children. A dragonfly lands on my finger. It seems all of nature responds to my love.

One day Frank calls me up from the basement.

"They're crossing through my garden. Right through the middle of it." He takes me out to the black cherry tree to point out the ten wild turkeys that are jerking across the lawn.

"Amazing."

He's still holding his gun. His screwy aim or eyesight or intention means he's never really hit anything. The next day, as we rattle out of Chatham on the way to my therapy appointment, Adam slams on the brakes. Ten, wild turkeys saunter across the road. I realise they are not in our garden. We are in theirs.

I ask Frank if I can garden for him. I want to earn my keep. Frank has an orchestra of horticulturalists tending to his estate. Sometimes they arrive in trucks with giant ladders that stretch above the trees. I become the weeder at the underbelly of the team. It is good for me, to sink my hands in the earth, in the roots, to shake it all up a bit. It's painful at first. Frank stands over me and tells me where to turn. I want to tackle him. He teaches me how to dig a hole. If he's not careful I'll dig him a grave and bury him. I wonder how a man with such success can crave so much reverence. The more my thoughts pull that out of the ground, the more its weeds spread around me. He mutters the word weed about ten times a minute, which isn't helping my decision to give up that habit.

"The trowel makes it much easier, I keep telling you."

I'm too embarrassed to tell him that I like the sensation of wet soil between my fingers and that I don't want to decapitate any earthworms. I pick up the trowel and probably truncate one when

Frank's mobile phone rings in his pocket.

"Dick! HAHAHAHA. You know it. What? Really. Touché. We'll get them to ship over another one."

He stumbles off, shouting into his hand. Poor, kind man with his gammy knee. I'd respect him if he hadn't leered over me when we first met. Dick's on the town committee with him. They're refurbishing the derelict cinema. He's not trying to condescend me. He doesn't think I'm a cretin. Maybe I do respect him. Maybe he just loves having a crew to direct, a creation to lead, and a project to manage. So do I. What am I doing on my knees? Did I throw my whole life away?

Weeds grow beneath me and tangle round my legs. They're already shooting up again by the oak tree and I haven't even made it past the smoking lounge. This is a ridiculous, endless job. Never done. Never finished. All these perfectly trim American lawns are beginning to annoy me. Let the jungle rise up and swallow us whole.

After a week, my mind quiets and I realise I like it here again, on the earth, on my knees. I'm enjoying myself, listening to the waves crash. Warblers hop along the branches beside me, yellow as buttercups. The rescue boat trundles by every hour. If I'll never get it done, why strain so hard? Look at the sea lions on the spit bathing like beach addicts. Who am I racing? The spring flowers are beginning to bud. Deep blue storm clouds congregate above us. The winking sun peeks through them, flooding the snowdrops in a silvery light that shoots through my eyes and bathes the garden in a dimension I've never seen before. It hits me with a thunderclap that these flowers are living masterpieces. They just grow out of the fucking ground. How had I never noticed before? Look at the colours for Christ's sake. What mixed them? What imagined that red? That white? That blue? How did those patterns just spring out of the stardust? Look at that

fucking blue tit. They just grow. It's a miracle. A squawk lifts my head up. Seven hawks are circling above me. Lightning forks the atmosphere. The sky opens and I'm soaked.

I'm watching the dragonflies dance. I feel like I've won a free ticket to the New York ballet, only it's better. Stephanie, the gardener, calls me over to her. From the orchard I've been observing her thick, wild movements as she digs up the earth with her buffalo strength. Her back looks solid as a tortoise shell. She was introduced to me as the chief. For the first time, I see her soft face, blushed like a rose. She needs a hand replanting the hydrangea bush. I ask her how long she's been the head gardener here.

"Nearly ten years for Mr. Mayer."

I hold up the trestle as she instructs me.

"And before that?"

"Oh the earth is one big garden. There's always someone in need."

"Where did you learn?"

"My father taught me when I was eight."

She doesn't seem interested in chatting so I try to remain silent. I smell the fecund earth in her hair. She's bent double, shaking the bush to set it free. I can't help myself.

"My father thought girls had no place on the land. To be fair, I did crash his quad into a wall. I was so euphoric I couldn't find the brake pedal."

I tense my weedy biceps to support the trestle as she uproots the whole thing.

"There's a rock underneath here you see. The roots are trapped.

She can't find nourishment."

She guides me to the hollow she's dug out. I walk backwards with the top end of the wilting plant.

"What's this oozy stuff?"

"Oh that's what the tendrils secrete to help them stick."

"It looks like cement."

"She's a clever thing, but it doesn't matter how high she climbs; she'll wither if she doesn't draw her strength from beneath."

I watch Stephanie transfer dozens of bright, new flowers from plastic tubs into the dark, moist soul of the beds. She might have buffalo strength, but she handles everything gently. A warbler lands beside me. I once had ideas and beliefs that climbed higher and higher and fixed like cement. Maybe it's time to tear down everything.

The dragonflies return and spiral as I work. Butterflies come in every colour of the rainbow. Stephanie disappears to the other pole of the garden. It's so far away that I can't see her. Occasionally I look up and watch the hawks gliding in circles high above me. Frank drives away in his cream, convertible Jaguar, waving with his roof down.

The flowers transform every day. There must be fifty different species in one bed alone. Each gives me a different sensation as I weed around them. Some bring passion and some softness. Others make me feel jubilation, wild frenzy and abandon. I sing them the songs that play through my headphones. Their leaves respond, unfurling softly and bending towards me. I feel they have fingertips that touch me, long invisible arms that wrap around me. It seems imperceptible but it's also clear as day. Often I think now I've gone and done it, gone bat-shit crazy, but I'm bursting with love.

I throw up my arms and say thank you to the light that bathed my whole life, and then the entire world comes out to play with me. Baby rabbits dart across the lawn.

"Run rabbits. Run."

I trundle in for some lunch. As I untie my shoes and wash my hands, I feel afraid of what I'll find in the basement.

"Weep motherfucker!"

Adam's playing Halo in the dark, congealing to the floor with the carpet picnic of cockroach shells and last year's pizza toppings.

"How's it going?"

"Oh you know. Just woke up. The usual. Migraine."

"Is it better since last night?"

He snorts.

"You know the script. Don't ask me if it's better. Ask me if it's less worse."

I go to greet the rats. They race out and climb on my shoulders. Their dinner still lies scattered there, uneaten. My beautiful mirrors. I puked up my own. This happens every time I decide that I can't bare to stay another day here. Adam is a pestilent moron who catalysed my tragic and irreversible demise. Poor fucking me. One thought leads to another and before I know it, my head is over the toilet bowl. Nothing makes one more helpless than giving the conditions of their happiness to another. Last night, I found the rats' food bowl hurled across the floor. They wouldn't come out to play with me.

I take the rats to Adam and place Blue on his head. Adam punches his chest and belches air. Balzac darts up the stairs. Blue follows.

"Arrrrghhhh. I can't get it out."

I lie on the floor. Blue and Balzac wrestle on my chest. Adam reaches around his feet and swallows two Excedrins.

"Adam, do you want to visit Salem?"

"Not really."

"How about Waltham? Emerson lived there. Apparently there's nice walks."

"Who?"

"Emerson."

"Yeh. Fuck him. Hahahaha. But seriously."

Blue slides off me and scrounges for the chocolate balls that missed Adam's bowl. Balzac scurries back to the cage.

Back in the garden, my fingers tear up the soil with snapping, angry, alligator thoughts of why Adam has ruined my mood and possibly my life. I can't feel the flowers anymore. They're as lifeless as dummies in a shop window display. The more I think he's a moron, the more he behaves like one. He doesn't want my love. I can't pull a fucking weed out. I give up and climb a tree. All these years I didn't listen to my body when the voice of negativity crept through me, like a poison that throbbed and choked my cells.

I stop in the graveyard on my way back from the pool. I was following a crow and she led me. A nice old lady asked me if I was half-dolphin. I'd like to be whole-dolphin. I prop the bicycle against a tree and sink my hands in my pockets. It's a frosty morning. Dewdrops lick the cobwebs. The gate is stiff. The crow flaps over my head and cawes. Another crow squawks back. I see her, black as night, on the pale shoulder of a stone angel.

Union Cemetery. I wonder how many died in union. I wonder

how many died in battle with their neighbours, their families, and themselves.

"Nancy, wife of Benjamin Beckwith. Died July 16, 1854. 72 years."

Tell me, Nancy. What did you do with your life? Did you truly know this man buried by your side? What mattered most when you took your final breath?

I wonder about the Wampanoag who danced on this dirt five hundred years before me, their descendents dancing still. I wonder what their ancestors would tell me. Would they teach me union? Would they show me how to trust and care and nourish community? How to listen to the heart and hear the land?

I must have left the gate open. The two crows are waiting by my bike. Back at the house I lie on the lawn with these ten thousand questions spinning round my mind. The bird song grows louder and the lapping of the waves, the swish of the grass stalks and the butterfly's wings. Then a voice above my left ear, a man's voice, deep and firm and loving, so distinct from the voice of my own thoughts I rediscover I'm not alone here, "Softer," he whispers. "Softer."

A voice is calling me. I follow her song out onto the sea rocks. As I cross the lawn I throw my arms out and run. A rabbit hops ahead of me. I knew this song when I was too young and playful to assume I had to navigate ten thousand critical manoeuvres on the chessboard of my life. Sky and sea are flushed in hues of violet, opal and mandarin, a rainbow stairway climbing into and out of the sun.

The grass knows the song and the rocks and the sea breeze. A nightingale greets me from the cedar tree. The wrens add bass and the scarlet cardinals a descant. A chorus collects in every branch and chirps the melody with gusto. The earthworms, clovers, and squirrels are all waking up and dancing to the great song of life. I slip on my trainers and run into the arms of the morning.

A little dachshund trots by my side behind the neighbour's white picket fence. Bright Indigo Buntings and red cardinals with mohawks flit, along with larks, doves, and tangerine birds that I don't know the name of. They all flutter across my path from the bushes. The cherry and peach trees burst with blossom and a starburst of blackbirds explodes from the round bush beneath the lighthouse. Seagulls hover like old sea captains above the little machines you put a silver coin in to gaze across the ocean. A hawk meets me at the mail boxes on the bend of Lover's Lake. He swoops a hair's breadth above me before disappearing into the forest. Up ahead, three more hawks perch still as statues on a telegraph wire, staring down at me as if they've been waiting. As I run beneath them I feel their feathers in my hair as they weave in a dance at the helm of my journey.

We glide onto the steep slope of Apple Tree Hill. They lead me or I lead them. I can't tell the difference. Over the precipice of the climb they soar away to join nine of their kin spiralling circles over Stage Island.

I find a path that cuts through the forest and follow them in a dance over wayward branches and rocks. I'm giddy with the way the light falls on the scrub oak when I see her. I think she must be an apparition. She stands serenely. Gracefully, waiting. Her hide is streaked with the star dust rays of the still-rising sun. I sway to a halt. The doe and I stand watching each other for minutes upon minutes. She doesn't move and I don't. My breath swirls towards her and vanishes. She seems to look inside me and show me back my nature. I have the sensation that she knows me more deeply than I have ever known myself. In the distance a woodpecker hammers at a tree. Gently, my friend tips her head to the side and trots on through the trees.

The hammering beats louder until I'm standing directly underneath it. I stop there and watch the little woodpecker in action. A crow swoops down and lands in the branch beside me. The branch bounces on my shoulder. Another crow caws and another. Six more land in the grotto, cooing wildly in a conversation I'm a part of yet can't fathom. More birds arrive—larks and wrens, cardinals and goldfinches. Dozens of them collect around me and join the cacophony.

I stand in the centre of this gathering, looking up at this kaleidoscopic dream, wondering what it means and if it has to mean anything. I decided it doesn't matter. I know how it feels.

bio

Gayle is a writer and artist based in Edinburgh, Scotland. She achieved her bachelor's degree in drama at Exeter University and her master's degree in fine arts in film directing at Edinburgh College of Art. She has worked in theatre, film and illustration. Gayle studied shamanism with shamans from Brazil, France and the United Kingdom and spent time healing with the Shipibo-Conibo healers of Peru. She is passionate about the transformative power of storytelling. *dancing with crows* is her first novel.